Military Pistols & Revolvers

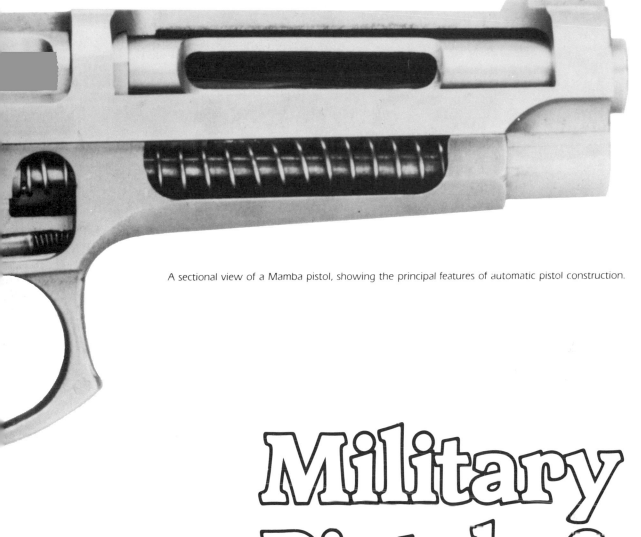

A sectional view of a Mamba pistol, showing the principal features of automatic pistol construction.

Military Pistols & Revolvers

IAN V. HOGG

ARMS AND ARMOUR PRESS

Acknowledgements Most of the photographs come from the author's collection, but I should like to thank the following for filling some of the gaps: Colt's, Inc., Hartford, Connecticut, USA (picture 1); Christie's, London (29); Weller & Dufty, Birmingham (41); Wallis & Wallis, Lewes (44); Fabrique Nationale SA, Herstal, Belgium (59, 97–9, 119–21); Remington Arms Co., Bridgeport, Connecticut, USA (62); Eidgenössische Waffenfabrik, Berne, Switzerland (74, 104); Mauser-Jagdwaffen GmbH, Oberndorf/Neckar, West Germany (110); Carl Walther GmbH, Ulm/Donau, West Germany (111); Heckler & Koch GmbH, Oberndorf/Neckar, West Germany (128–31); Pietro Beretta SpA, Gardone Val Trompia, Italy (135–8); Astra-Unceta y Cia, Guernica, Spain (140); SIG, Neuhausen/Rheinfalls, Switzerland (142–3); Smith & Wesson, Springfield, Massachusetts, USA (144); and John Walter, for pictures of guns in the collection of Dr Rolf Gminder (12, 37, 39, 40, 109) and the Savage (65).

First published in Great Britain in 1987 by Arms and Armour Press Ltd., Link House, West Street, Poole, Dorset BH15 1LL.

Distributed in the USA by Sterling Publishing Co. Inc., 2 Park Avenue, New York, NY 10016.

Distributed in Australia by Capricorn Link (Australia) Pty. Ltd., P.O. Box 665, Lane Cove, New South Wales 2066, Australia.

British Library Cataloguing in Publication Data:
Hogg, Ian V.
Military pistols and revolvers.
1. Armed forces – Equipment – History
2. Pistols – History
I. Title
623.4'43'09034   UD410
ISBN 0-85368-807-9

Designed by David Gibbons; edited by Michael Boxall; typeset by Typesetters (Birmingham) Ltd., printed and bound in Great Britain by The Bath Press, Avon.

Jacket illustration: one of the many competitors in the military marketplace, the 9mm Steyr GB, a modern gas-delayed blowback design with an unusually large magazine capacity (Courtesy of Steyr-Daimler-Puch AG)

CONTENTS

INTRODUCTION

In 1968 there was a Firearms Amnesty in Great Britain, and shortly afterwards I found myself travelling round British police stations in the company of the armourer of the Royal Military College of Science, examining the weapons and ammunition which had been handed in. There were some remarkable things to be seen and one byproduct of this was that I had the idea to write a small book illustrating the wide variety of military pistols and revolvers which had seen service during the twentieth century. This was my first book, and it was published by the Arms & Armour Press in 1970. It was a slender paperback selling for fifteen shillings (75p for those with short memories). Although long out of print in Britain, it has continued to sell in foreign countries ever since, albeit in small numbers.

In 1985 Mr Lionel Leventhal, who originally agreed to publish the book, suggested that perhaps it was time that it was brought up to date and expanded into a more narrative form, covering the general history of military handguns. This book is the result, and I hope it finds as receptive a readership as did the original. It is obviously impossible to cover every pistol that has found its way into the hands of soldiers throughout history, and therefore I have had to confine the story to the most significant weapons. Moreover I have been ruthless in excluding several pistols which, though of the requisite calibre and characteristics, have never been officially adopted for military service or are not of sufficient novelty to warrant inclusion on technical grounds. If, therefore, you feel that something has been overlooked, I apologise but would suggest that it probably never received any official blessing. I also apologise for the fact that we have been unable to do this one for fifteen shillings.

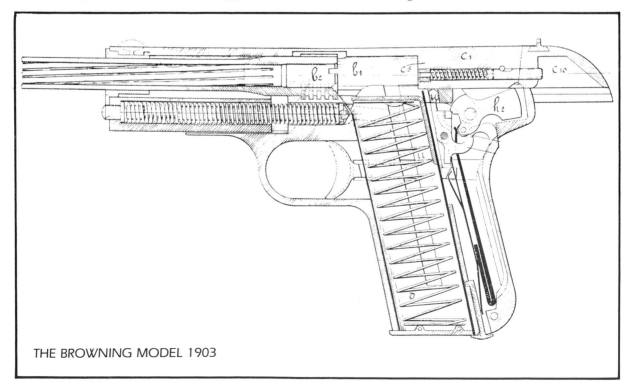

THE BROWNING MODEL 1903

1

THE REVOLVER IN NINETEENTH-CENTURY MILITARY SERVICE

The military forces of the world had taken little note of any type of repeating arm before the early years of the nineteenth century. This was not military conservatism; it was plain common sense. In the days of flintlocks, powder and ball, the idea of a repeating weapon, though touted from time to time, was grossly impractical. It is true that flintlock revolvers had been made, but these were of considerable precision and expense, and far beyond the capacity of any organized military force to purchase and maintain in good repair.

It was the arrival of the percussion system of firing, and particularly of the percussion cap, that began to make repeating arms slightly more practicable, but it seems probable, in the absence of other data, that the first attempt to interest a military force in a revolving pistol was that made by E. H. Collier with his revolver in 1819.

Collier, an American, had developed a flint-lock revolver, using ideas communicated to him by a Captain Wheeler. It was an ingenious invention, using a torsion spring to rotate the cylinder and a compression spring to force the cylinder tightly into engagement with the barrel before discharge, so limiting the escape of gas at the chamber/barrel joint. In 1818 he came to England to secure a patent, and in 1819 he submitted the weapon to the Duke of Wellington for test. The Duke ordered a Board of Officers to convene at Woolwich and the test was carried out. In his report, the Commanding Officer at Woolwich observed that while it was 'very ingenious', nevertheless it was 'by far too complicated and expensive to be applicable to the Public Service'. Collier persisted, however, and a further test, this time of a rifle using the same principle, was carried out in 1824. Again, the testing board admitted it to be a clever and accurate weapon, but that was as far as it was prepared to go. Collier gave up his hope of military adoption, and thereafter confined his efforts to the commercial market, where he met with some success.

In 1835 Samuel Colt appeared on the scene. Colt, born in 1814, had a somewhat varied career. Although coming from a prosperous family, at the age of sixteen he went to sea as a cabin-boy. In later years the infant public relations industry fabricated a romantic tale of how he had watched the ship's wheel and, inspired by it, whittled a working revolver from scrap wood; there seems to be little ground for this tale. He left the sea and next appeared in the mid-West as 'Doctor Coult', purveyor of patent medicines, making a living from these and from titillating the yokels by administering laughing-gas. But throughout this period he undoubtedly had some interest in firearms design, and in 1832, after amassing sufficient money, he went to Anson Chase, a New England mechanic, and expounded his ideas. Chase made him a few specimen revolvers which appear to have been somewhat crude — at least one is said to have exploded when first fired. In 1834 Colt found a better workman in John Pearson of Baltimore who managed to produce precisely what Colt had envisaged. Colt set sail for England and took out Patent 6909 on 22 October 1835, then returned to America to take out Patent 9430X on 25 February 1836. He was 21 years old.

Patent 9430X was a 'master patent' insofar as it prevented anyone else from making a revolver using a mechanical system for rotating the cylinder. Colt's system used a hand or pawl attached to the hammer, together with a cylinder bolt which firmly locked the cylinder in place while the shot was fired, but freed it for the pawl to operate when the trigger was released. But the wording of the patent effectively shut out any other method of operation and gave Colt a monopoly on revolver manufacture which was to last for 21 years.

Colt set up his Patent Firearms Manufacturing Company in Paterson, New Jersey, and made pistols, rifles, shotguns and carbines, but sales were slow, his financial backer went bankrupt, and in 1842 the company closed

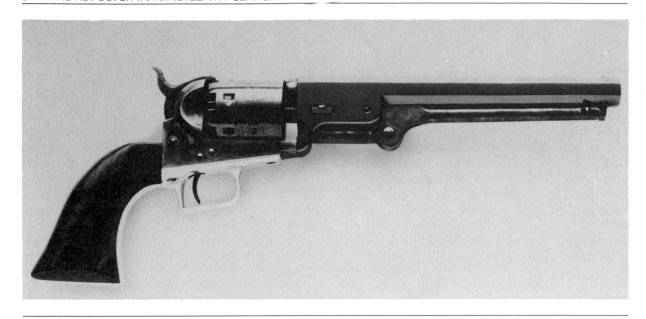

1. The .36 Colt Navy model revolver, also known as the Model of 1851, was one of the most widely distributed of all the cap-and-ball designs – so successful, in fact, that Colt's still makes the modern replica shown here.

down. There was, in fact, little demand for firearms in the USA at that time. Four years later, though, the Mexican War broke out and the firearms business began to look up. Major-General Zachary Taylor, commanding the US force in Mexico, was impressed by the Colt revolvers carried by a number of his officers and sent Captain Samuel Walker to see Colt and arrange for the manufacture of a revolver for military use. Walker suggested some improvements, Colt put together a design, an order for 1,000 was placed, and Colt, having no factory, went to Eli Whitney, Jr, a well-known arms maker in New Haven, Connecticut, and persuaded him to manufacture the new pistol. Another order for 1,000 pistols followed, and on the proceeds of these two orders Colt was able to set up his own factory once more.

Colt's basic design, known today as the 'Paterson' Colt, was of the type now called 'open frame'; the butt and frame of the revolver were separate from the barrel unit, which fastened on to the front of the frame and was locked by a wedge. This meant that the cylinder top was exposed, there being no connection (or 'top strap') between the standing breech behind the cylinder and the barrel. It was percussion fired, with nipples at the rear end of

each chamber of the five-shot cylinder, was loaded with powder and ball, and was of .34in calibre. The trigger folded up beneath the frame when not in use, but thumbing back the hammer to full-cock automatically dropped the trigger into the firing position. To reload, it was necessary to pull out the wedge, remove the barrel, and slip the cylinder from its arbor; users generally found it more convenient to carry a spare loaded cylinder ready to slip back on to the arbor and then replace the barrel and wedge. In 1839 Colt patented a lever rammer which allowed the chambers to be loaded with the cylinder in place on the pistol.

The 'Walker' Colt, designed on Walker's recommendations, was a much heavier weapon of .44 calibre, with a 9-inch barrel and a six-shot cylinder. It also used a fixed trigger and a trigger guard, but it was still a single-action weapon, needing to be thumb-cocked before the trigger could be pressed. Subsequent models – including the Dragoon and Pocket Models of 1848, the Navy Model of 1851, the Army Model of 1860 and the Police Model of 1862 – were little more than reduced versions of the Walker model.

Although the Mexican War was soon over, Colt was lucky in that the California gold rush of 1849 came along as his military contracts were drying up. All the pioneers demanded firearms, and the success of Colt's pistol in Mexico gave it a cachet of reliability; thousands were sold, so that in 1855 Colt could open a new factory in Hartford, Connecticut.

Before then, though, he had returned to Britain to exhibit his revolvers and rifles at the Great Exhibition of 1851. At that time the revolver was a novelty in Britain, and his exhibit aroused considerable interest. He approached the British Government, and a trial of Colt's .44 Dragoon, in competition with the only English competitor, the Deane & Adams pistol, took place in September 1851. Encouraged by this, Colt opened a factory in London, since his existing Hartford factory was finding it difficult to manufacture weapons fast enough for the American market without thinking about export. Eventually, in March 1854, the Royal Navy ordered 4,000 of Colt's Model 1851 'Navy' revolvers, followed by a further order for 5,500 later in the year. Early in 1855 a further 5,000 were ordered for the British Army, and this was followed by an order for another 9,000 in August 1855.

The Colt revolver had won its acceptance into the British Army largely on two counts: its accuracy, and the interchangeability of parts. At that time most gunmaking was done by skilled workmen who 'fettled' each component to a perfect fit with the remainder; Colt took the art out of gunmaking and turned it into a simple mechanical routine, producing standardized parts by machine to tightly controlled dimensions, so that assembly simply became a matter of picking the necessary pieces out of bins and putting them together, a task which could be performed by relatively unskilled workers. But for practical use in the field, the Colt was frequently considered, by soldiers, to be inferior to a British design, the Deane & Adams revolver, since this was far more robust.

The Deane & Adams, as we have said, was Colt's only competitor at the 1851 Exhibition, and it was generally found at any demonstration or competition in which the Colt revolver figured, since Deane was an astute business man and could see the advantages of military adoption. It differed considerably from the Colt design in two major features: first, it was a solid frame' revolver – the barrel and frame were milled from a single piece of steel, with a

2. The .450 'Pistol, Adams', B.L., Revolver, Mark II' was introduced in 1872 and finally declared obsolete in August 1894.

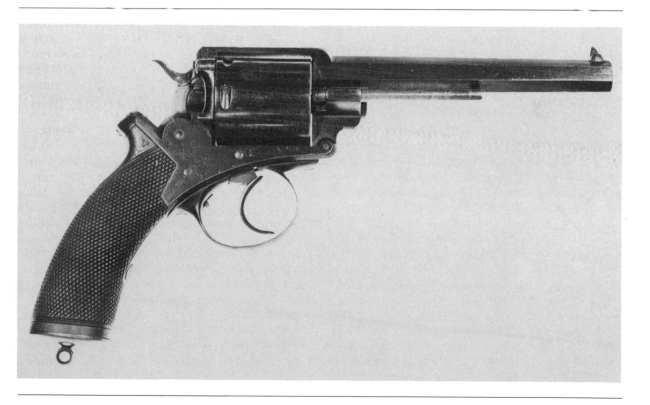

rectangular hole in the centre into which the cylinder fitted and was retained by a central pin or arbor. Secondly, the hammer was cocked and released by a single pull of the trigger; there was, indeed, no way of thumbing back the hammer since there was no hammer spur.

The solid frame made the Adams revolver far more robust under active service conditions, while the 'self-cocking' trigger made it faster to fire. On the debit side, the interchangeability feature did not exist, it was rather harder to keep clean, and the self-cocking trigger meant a stiff pull which tended to throw off the aim and thus it generally showed as being less accurate in deliberate fire than was the Colt.

Robert Adams, the inventor of the revolver, was aware of these drawbacks, and although his pistols sold quite well, he was looking for some way of besting Colt. He found his answer in a Lieutenant Beaumont of the Royal Engineers who, in February 1855, patented a novel design of trigger mechanism which allowed the hammer to be thumb-cocked to give 'single action' working, or could be self-cocked and fired by a single pull of the trigger if the firer so wished. Thus, for deliberate fire the single action was used, while in an emergency the self-cocking feature was available. This became the 'double action' lock mechanism which has been used in revolvers ever since.

In March 1855, the Board of Ordnance tested the Beaumont-Adams design. This was remarkably speedy, since the patent had not yet been granted even though applications dated back to December of the previous year; before the year was out an order for 2,000 revolvers had been placed. Two types were eventually adopted: one in 54 bore (about .38in) with a 6-inch barrel, and one in 38 bore (about .45in) with a 7.5-inch barrel. Both were six-shot percussion weapons and they remained in service until about 1870, orders for several thousand more being placed throughout the intervening years – indeed, the Adams was not declared obsolete until 1894.

By this time the muzzle-loading cap-and-ball revolver was in its last days; the breech-loading metallic cartridge had arrived and was about to take over. Its first military application came with the pinfire cartridge attributed to Casimir Lefaucheux, a French gunmaker. Houllier had invented the cartridge in 1846, after which Lefaucheux produced a suitable shotgun to

chamber it. The latter then refined the cartridge, taking out patents of his own in 1850. The principle called for a metallic base and cardboard body containing the powder and shot, together with a percussion cap inside the base. Resting on this cap was a metal pin which protruded from the side of the base. The weapon was breech loaded and a slot in the chamber permitted the end of the pin to stand proud of the barrel when the gun was closed. A conventional hammer fell when the trigger was pressed, striking the pin and thus firing the cap inside the cartridge.

The basic idea was refined by a number of inventors until by the 1850s it had become a one-piece metallic cartridge capable of carrying shot or of being fitted with a bullet, and in 1854 Lefaucheux's son, Eugène, patented a pinfire revolver. It was a single-action open-frame weapon with a push-rod beneath the barrel to eject the spent cartridges from the chambers. After comparative trials of various revolvers, the French Navy adopted the Lefaucheux pinfire in 1856. They were rapidly followed by the Spanish Army and Italian Navy in 1858, the Danish Navy in 1861, Norwegian Navy in 1864 and the Swedish Army a year later. By 1865 the double-action trigger had been adopted. Most of the service pistols were in 11mm calibre, but the design was rapidly copied by innumerable French and Belgian gunmakers in calibres ranging from 7mm to 12mm.

In 1857, Colt's master patent expired, and was immediately superseded by another master patent, this time held by two names to become famous in handgun design, Horace Smith and Daniel Wesson. Smith and Wesson had worked for numerous companies and were expert gunsmiths and, in the early 1850s, seeing that Colt's patent was soon to expire, they had begun work on a new design of revolver. Having seen the power which Colt's patent had given, they carefully examined all the relevant patents then in existence and discovered that Rollin White, an ex-employee of Colt's, held a patent which, among several other relatively useless items, covered the simple principle of boring chambers completely through the cylinder so as to permit loading from the rear. He had offered this to Colt, but Colt must have had an off day, missed the point, and turned it down. Smith & Wesson snapped it up, and on extremely

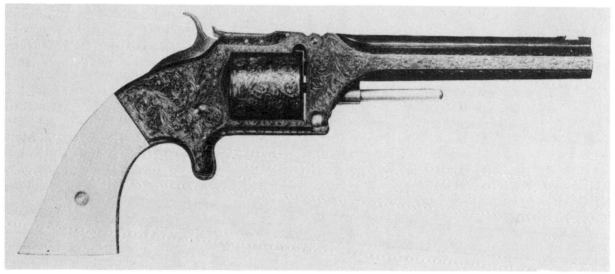

advantageous terms; White would receive a royalty on every revolver made, but would bear the cost of any litigation arising from attempts to copy the patent. It turned out that would-be pirates abounded and most of White's profits from the royalties were dissipated in legal expenses. (He eventually got out of the firearms business and patented a sewing-machine which made him a sizeable fortune.) From 1855, the date of the White patent, to 1869 no breech-loading revolver was successfully made in the USA without Smith & Wesson's permission.

What Smith & Wesson needed to make their idea work was a suitable cartridge, and they

3. Smith & Wesson First Model .22 revolver, showing the 'tip-up' method of construction.

4. Smith & Wesson 'Old Model No. 2' in an ornately engraved finish.

adopted the rimfire system. This, again, was a French invention, having first been devised by Flobert in about 1845, when he (in effect) put a small lead ball in the mouth of a percussion cap. In 1854 Smith & Wesson patented a cartridge in which the priming composition was held inside the folded rim (it also spread across the base of the case and it took them some time to perfect a manufacturing method whereby the cartridge case was spun during the insertion of the priming so as to put it in the rim and nowhere else) and a lead bullet was inserted into the mouth over a small powder charge. This was first made in .22 calibre and, indeed, survives today, in improved form, as the .22 Short cartridge. Production of their revolver began in 1857 and they were soon manufacturing them in large numbers, with other calibres coming along in the fullness of time.

When the American Civil War began in 1861 the hands of the Union purchasing authorities were tied by a law passed in 1860 which prohibited the purchase of 'arms of a patented character'. This law was designed to ensure that arms were obtained only from military manufactories, they being cheaper than commercial makers who had to charge a price reflecting overheads, taxes and a fair profit. Needless to say, once the war had begun it became obvious that the required numbers of pistols and other weapons were not to be forthcoming from the government arsenals, and the law was rapidly repealed. Now the way was open to purchase pistols from anyone, and the variety of weapons employed by both the Union and Confederate sides was limited only by the availability of sources. Some 146,000 Colt revolvers in .36 and .44 calibres were purchased officially by the Federal Government during the course of the war, while numbers were acquired by the Confederates, and unlicensed copies were made by several companies in the South as well as a few in the North after Colt's patents had expired.

More than 125,000 Remington revolvers were purchased by the Union forces; these were cap-and-ball weapons, using a solid frame, and were probably more robust than the Colt design. As and when available, Deane & Adams percussion and other European revolvers were purchased by both sides.

Statistically the third most important of the revolvers purchased on behalf of the Federal Government was the Starr, rather more than 47,000 of which were acquired during the Civil War. Patented (No. 14,118) by Ebenezer Starr in January 1856, with improvements in 1860, the popular .44 Starr Army Revolver – made in Yonkers and Binghamton, New York State – featured a double-action lock. The revolver weighed a little under 3lb, had a 6-inch barrel and measured about 11.6 inches overall. A few single-action guns were made, as were a few .36 calibre Navy guns; these, however, are rare compared with the standard version.

One of the most remarkable pistols to be adopted was the Confederates' 'Grapeshot Pistol' (to quote the official title), more generally called the Le Mat revolver. The Le Mat was designed by Dr F. A. Le Mat, a French-born American, who seems to have had little warrant for his doctorate. In 1856 he patented a percussion revolver in which the cylinder arbor took the form of a hollow tube from which a charge of shot could be fired. The hammer could be

5. The .44 Remington New Model Army Revolver, introduced in 1858, was one of the best of the cap-and-ball revolvers used during the American Civil War. About 125,000 were made, making the design second only to the Colts.

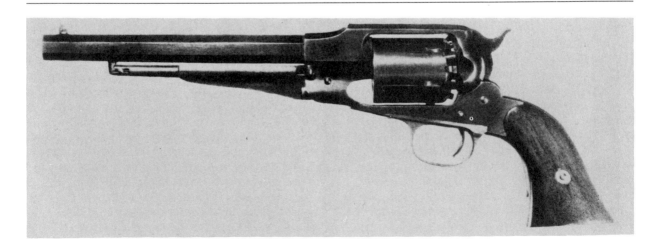

adjusted to fire the normal pistol cylinders, or to fire the shot charge. A number were made in New Orleans in 1860, but at the outbreak of the war Le Mat went to Paris to organize manufacture in quantity for the Confederate Army. The first batch was found to be so badly made that Le Mat took his business to England, and subsequently had the pistols made in Birmingham. The first models were 9-chambered, with the pistol barrel of .40 calibre and the shot barrel in 18 bore. In later years he modified the design to fire first pinfire and then centre-fire cartridges, and the pistol continued to sell into the 1870s.

The rimfire cartridge, as adopted by Smith & Wesson, gradually increased in size until .44 became a common calibre for both pistols and rifles. Nevertheless, it had its drawbacks. The principal one was that the metal of the case had to be sufficiently soft to permit being crushed by the falling hammer, so allowing the ignition composition to be properly fired. By inference, it followed that the metal was too soft to with-stand high pressures, and thus a really powerful cartridge in rimfire was out of the question, since under extreme pressure the cartridge metal would fail and allow gas to escape. This, in fact, was of little consequence to pistol manufacturers, since the pressure generated in revolvers was relatively small, but there was, at that time, a tendency to develop pistols and rifles or carbines of the same chambering so that a man could go to war or to the wilderness with short and long weapons and use the same ammunition in both. The obvious move was to try and develop ammunition which would give good performance in the rifle and then build the revolver strong enough to suit, but the rimfire at least had the advantage of limiting the pressure and performance and thus the size of revolvers.

6. The Le Mat cap-and-ball 'grapeshot' revolver, which featured a large-calibre smoothbore barrel doubling as the cylinder axis pin, originally patented in 1856. This is one of the later metallic cartridge guns, introduced a decade later.

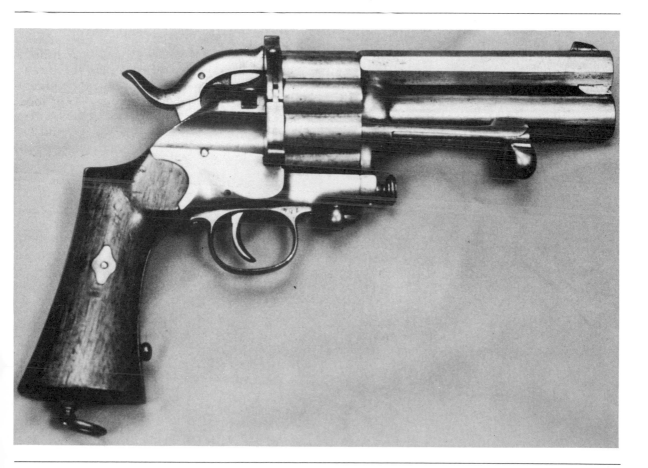

As a result of this deficiency in the rimfire, the central-fire cartridge was gradually perfected; it is no part of our study to examine all the various types of central-fire cartridge which were put forward and we can thus go straight to the final form. This was a metallic case, with an upstanding rim at the rear to facilitate extraction of the empty case, and with a percussion cap mounted centrally in the base where it was readily struck by a falling hammer. The first cases were often of compound construction, using brass or iron bases with paper or card bodies, or iron bases with wrapped brass bodies, but these all showed defects and were soon relegated to history by the universal perfection of the one-piece drawn brass case. Once this type of ammunition became common, in the late 1860s, the designers of revolvers were able to go ahead and assimilate their designs to the new type of cartridge.

The principal problem which faced the revolver designer was simply the matter of getting the empty cases out of the cylinder and loading it with fresh cartridges in a convenient and speedy manner. The Smith & Wesson rimfire revolver and many other early designs used the simplest possible solution – they removed the cylinder entirely, either by 'breaking open' the frame (as in the original Smith & Wesson 'tip-up' revolvers) or by simply removing the arbor pin and allowing the cylinder to drop from the frame. Once removed the cylinder could be loaded and replaced; after being fired it was removed and the cases punched out one by one. The Smith & Wesson had a heavy pin mounted in the frame beneath the barrel for this purpose, while most European designs simply used the arbor pin for the task. As might be imagined, it was a slow business and, as with the early Colt and other cap-and-ball percussion revolvers, it became normal practice to carry a spare, fully loaded cylinder which could replace the fired one when time was of the essence.

The first improvement on this system was the idea of 'gate loading', generally attributed to a Belgian gunsmith called Abadie. If he did invent the idea, he must either have failed to patent it or drawn up a faulty patent, since within a very short time it was in use throughout the world. In the gate-loading system a section of the standing breech, behind the

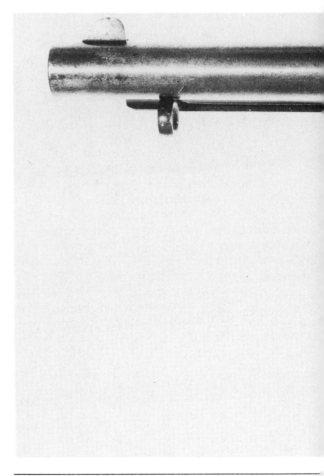

cylinder, is arranged to hinge outwards so as to expose one of the chambers on one side of the cylinder – usually the right side. The hammer was provided with a 'half-cock' notch so that it could be drawn back clear of the chambers and so withdraw the cylinder bolt. This enabled the cylinder to be rotated freely, and with the gate open the chambers could be loaded one by one, the cylinder being moved round until all the chambers were filled. The gate was then closed and the hammer drawn back to full cock, after which firing could commence.

Once the contents of the cylinder had been fired, it became necessary to remove the empty cases. Once more the hammer was half-cocked and the gate opened, and a rod, attached to a hinged arm, withdrawn from its resting-place inside the cylinder arbor. The arm was swung across so that the rod aligned with the chamber opposite the opened gate, and by pushing back the rod the empty case was ejected. The rod

7. The Colt Single Action Army Revolver – alias the Model 1873, Peacemaker, Frontier, Thumb-buster, Hogleg and a good many other names as well.

was withdrawn, the cylinder revolved to the next chamber, the rod pushed again, and so on until all the cases were out and reloading could begin.

It was soon discovered that there was one slight defect in this system; with careless handling it was far too easy to allow the hammer to drop on a loaded chamber while still in the process of loading, and the resulting discharge could be hazardous to bystanders or even the person doing the loading. Abadie quickly came up with an answer to this: linking the hammer to the loading gate, so that as the gate was opened a shaped cam would push the hammer back sufficiently to free the cylinder bolt. So long as the gate remained open the cam remained in place, effectively preventing the hammer moving forward.

The gate-loading system had the merit of being simple, easy to use, and having very little that could go wrong with it. The other side of

the coin was the slow business of poking out the individual cases and inserting the individual cartridges, revolving the cylinder between each operation, and it was little wonder that many gate-loading revolvers still had quick-release arbor pins so that the entire cylinder could be slipped from the frame and replaced with a loaded cylinder when quick reloading was demanded. But the simplicity outweighed much else, and gate-loading revolvers are still to be found in present-day manufacture, principally in cheap small-calibre weapons, but also in heavy-calibre models based on the most famous gate-loader of all, the Colt Model 1873 'Frontier' or 'Army Model' or 'Peacemaker', to give it but three of its names.

After exploring a blind alley in the guise of the tapering, rimless front-loading Thuer centre-fire cartridge, Colt's had gone into the cartridge era, once the Smith & Wesson master patent expired, with what was little more than a .44 rimfire version of their original open-top frame design. This appeared in 1871 with the intention of obtaining a military contract, despite the fact that the US Army had, in 1868, declared that it wanted a solid-frame model. Not surprisingly the Model of 1871 was a failure, but in 1873 this failure was redeemed when the Model 1873 appeared. This was a solid-frame, gate-loaded, single-action revolver which is instantly recognizable as the archetypal 'Colt'. It was adopted by the US Army in the summer of 1873 and it went on to become virtually a symbol of America. Production began in 1873 and continued, without a break, until 1940, during which period 357,389 had been made. A few were completed from spares just after the end of the Second World War, but then came a ten-year break when the Colt company tried to dissociate itself from this obsolete weapon. But public demand persisted, foreign copies began to proliferate, and in self-defence Colt began manufacture again in 1955. Originally in .45 calibre, the Model 1873 was eventually chambered for thirty different cartridges, from the humble .22 rimfire at one end of the scale to the .476 Enfield at the other. And in addition to these stock calibres, it has been possible to have the weapon chambered for any other cartridge desired, so long as the gun could withstand it.

Even though the Model 1873 prospered, there were still complaints about gate loading; some people shrugged them off – if you couldn't hit your man with six shots, you were in trouble anyway – but in military situations there were distinct advantages to be gained by quicker reloading. One system, which saw a variety of mechanical attempts, was to link some form of ejector with the hammer, so that as the hammer fell on the loaded chamber it flipped out the fired cartridge from the previous chamber. This appeared on an Austrian design in 1880, was tried in Britain in 1884 with the Silver & Fletcher ejector, but only ever gained military acceptance on a Swiss revolver in 1882. Like many other firearms inventions, the automatic ejector usually worked well enough in the

workshop or the showroom, but it tended to be less than efficient in the field.

The system relied on two prime factors: first, that the weapon and its ammunition were spotlessly clean and perfectly lubricated, and secondly that the cartridge cases were of correct dimensions and of the same ductility from round to round. If the weapon were stiff, if the hammer axis was badly lubricated, if dirt were present in the chamber, or if the cartridge case was slightly oversize or the metal softer than usual, either the hammer failed to generate sufficient power as it fell or the case put up more resistance to being ejected. The fact that the case refused to eject was no life-or-death matter, since it could always be extracted by some other method (there was usually a conventional ejector rod on the pistol), but the tight case meant that the ejector arm failed to move properly under the blow of the hammer, and therefore it prevented the hammer delivering the correct force of blow to the cap of the chamber about to be fired. So not only did it fail to eject, it also failed to fire. The Silver & Fletcher design attempted to mitigate this disaster by allowing the ejector to be disengaged, so that the revolver could be fired normally, then brought into action so that half-a-dozen 'dry' operations of the hammer would eject all the spent cases, but even with this refinement automatic ejectors were never popular.

Another reason why the automatic ejector failed to prosper was simply that something better had appeared. In 1870, Smith & Wesson, who were now being given a run for their money by a score of pistol makers in the USA, brought out their classic '.44 American' revolver and introduced a new method of extraction. The frame of the .44 American had a prominent hinge bolt below and ahead of the cylinder, about which the entire barrel, cylinder and top strap unit could be swung downwards. A simple spring catch held the top strap to the standing breech while the revolver was being fired; after releasing this catch the barrel was swung down and a cam on the hinge bolt pressed in a rod which passed through the cylinder arbor. At the rear end of this rod was a star-shaped plate which normally sat in a recessed portion of the cylinder and formed the inside edges of the chambers, upon which the extracting rim of the cartridges rested. As the barrel went down so the cam forced the rod and the star-shaped ejector plate backwards, and this pushed the empty cartridge cases out of the chambers and allowed them to fall to the ground. Further depression of the barrel allowed the ejector plate to snap back into place in the cylinder ready for reloading. The enormous leverage which could be applied by pressing down the long barrel meant that even the stiffest cartridge case could be forced out of the dirtiest chamber, and with the entire rear end of the chamber exposed, reloading was very quick and easy.

Smith & Wesson produced this revolver in 1870; in the following year Colt's produced their Open Top .44 Rimfire model, and one would expect that S&W would have captured the market. That they did not, and that the Colt became the symbol of the American West rather than the .44 American forms a peculiar tale.

Several prominent citizens had adopted the .44 American, among them Wyatt Earp, 'Buffalo Bill' Cody and (probably) Wild Bill Hickok. Shortly after the pistol had been introduced, the Russian Army decided to adopt a revolver to arm its cavalry and artillery soldiers and sent a mission to the USA to select a suitable weapon. According to legend the Grand Duke heading the mission went hunting with Buffalo Bill and was impressed by his proficiency with the .44 American. The accuracy of the weapon failed to

impress him quite so much, since it was far below the standards demanded by European armies due to a poorly designed bullet. So the Grand Duke's technical staff redesigned the entire cartridge, opening out the mouth of the case to take a slightly thicker and heavier bullet which gave an improvement of about 100 feet per second in velocity and also a considerable improvement in accuracy. With this settled, the Russians then asked Smith & Wesson if they could make a few small changes in the design of the revolver: a small spur on the grip so that the pistol butt did not slip through the hand on recoil when fired, a finger-rest beneath the trigger guard, and a 6.5-inch barrel. Smith & Wesson agreed to make these changes, the Russians tried them and pronounced them good, and forthwith gave the company an order for 215,704 revolvers.

This, of course, was the sort of order which, even today, pistol manufacturers dream about. In plain terms it meant turning out 175 revolvers a day for five years. and this single order kept the company so busy that they had to neglect the home commercial market, and this was Colt's opportunity. They produced their Model 1873 and the rest is history, although, from the technical point of view, the Colt 'Peacemaker' was a far inferior design to the

8. The Smith & Wesson .44 Russian Model, which made the company's fortune but cost it the US domestic market for many years.

'.44 Russian', as the Smith & Wesson design had now become.

This adoption of a revolver by the Russians stirred several European nations to look to their armouries. In Germany the famous rifle-maker, Peter Paul Mauser, decided to produce a military revolver, assuming that anything made by the army's rifle supplier would have an automatic edge on any competitor. In an attempt to develop a new and reliable system of revolving the cylinder, he produced the design which, ever since, has been known as the 'Mauser Zig-Zag'. This was a hinged-frame revolver in which the barrel hinged upwards rather than down, and the exterior of the cylinder was cut with grooves in a zigzag pattern. These grooves engaged with a pin, in the frame of the revolver, which was connected to the trigger mechanism. When the trigger was pulled (or the hammer cocked – it was a double-action lock) the pin moved back and, because of the inclination of

9, 10. The Mauser 'Zig-Zag' revolver, patented in 1878. Note the extraordinary way the gun opens for loading.

11. The solid but utterly unremarkable German 'Reichsrevolver' of 1883, generally (but erroneously) known as the 'Officers' Model'.

the groove, caused the cylinder to turn through one-sixth of a complete rotation and thus bring a chamber into line with the hammer. After the hammer fell and fired the cartridge, the next cocking movement moved the cylinder round again to line up the next chamber. After all the cartridges had been fired, pressure on a lever beneath the cylinder and frame opened the frame catch and the barrel could be hinged upwards. After opening widely it stopped, but continued pressure on the lever now forced out a central star ejector which cleared the chambers of the empty cases.

As with all Mauser products, then or now, it was an impeccable design and beautifully finished, but it failed to make its mark with the military; too complicated, they said, not to be put in the hands of the brutal and licentious soldiery. Let us, instead, appoint a Commission to produce a more suitable design.

Throughout the history of firearms there are a number of designs which have come to fruition as the result of Commissions of one sort or another; they all have one thing in common, and that is mediocrity. The Commission Revolver, or Reichsrevolver Model 1879, is no

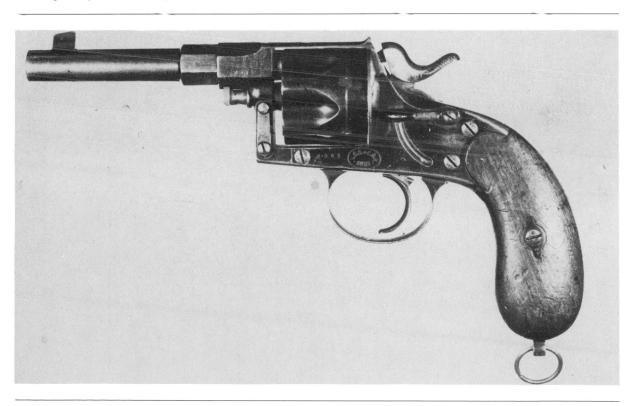

exception. Conceived at a time when technical innovation was lying around in all directions, it is remarkable for its primitive design; it is as if the Commission had never seen any revolver for the past ten years. A solid-framed, single-action design, it was gate-loaded from the right-hand side but, surprisingly, there was no ejector rod or other provision for removing the spent cases. The user had to remove the arbor pin, take out the cylinder, and then use the arbor pin to punch out the empties. Built in two models, the 1879 Troopers' Model with a 180mm barrel and the 1883 Officers' Model with 125mm barrel, the Reichsrevolver was chambered for 10.6mm centre-fire cartridges. Primitive it was, but robust – which was probably uppermost in the Commission's consideration – and numbers were to be found in the hands of rear-echelon troops as late as 1945.

The French, feeling that their open-frame Lefaucheux revolvers were now somewhat out of date, applied to the gun trade for a replacement and eventually selected a Chamelot-Delvigne design in 11mm centre-fire calibre. This was a solid-frame, gate-loaded, rod-ejecting, double-action revolver which was robust and simple, and it was basically a design used by many European countries. Chamelot-Delvigne refers to the design of the lockwork, and where the name came from is in some doubt since it was actually patented by a gunmaker called Pirlot. The result was that guns bearing the Chamelot-Delvigne name were made by any number of manufacturers, and the French revolver was turned out by several contractors before settling down under state control at the national armoury, the Manufacture Nationale d'Armes de Saint-Etienne. The Belgians adopted an 11mm design in 1871, the Swiss a 10.4mm rimfire in 1872, the Dutch a 9.4mm in 1873 and the Italians adopted a 10.4mm in 1879. All being more or less to the same design, it can be difficult to tell one from another without close examination.

12. The Italian Army's Chamelot-Delvigne style revolver, Mo.1872.

13. A French, commercial-pattern Chamelot-Delvigne revolver, essentially similar to the Mle 1874 officers' pattern.

14. The Chamelot-Delvigne inspired Italian Army revolver of 1889, better known as the 'Bodeo', remained in production until after the end of the First World War. Guns such as this one were made with folding triggers for police use.

In 1879 the British Army found itself short of revolvers, and in March of that year had to purchase a mixed bag from industry to fill an order for 500; and 100 of those had to be sent back to the makers to have various defects rectified. The Director of Artillery, responsible for armaments at that time, felt it unreasonable that in an emergency the Army had to go to three different manufacturers in order to acquire 500 revolvers, and even more unreasonable that 20 per cent of them should be defective. Accordingly, in July he asked the Royal Small Arms Factory at Enfield to design a revolver suitable for the army and navy. In just sixteen days the factory produced drawings and had them approved, and within five months the first pre-production models were being tested. Some small adjustments were made, and in August 1880 the design was approved as the 'Pistol, Revolver, Breech Loading, Enfield Mark I'.

The Enfield Mark I was a six-shot, double-action, hinged-frame weapon with a most curious extraction system. The barrel hinged downwards, but the cylinder remained parallel with the frame and was merely pulled forward. As it moved, so a fixed extracting star plate in the centre of the cylinder remained stationary, so that the cylinder was actually drawn over the empty cartridge cases. The only difficulty was that the bottom case usually managed to jam between the extracting plate and the bottom of the frame, and the operator had to give the cylinder a quick twist to clear it before beginning to reload. Another interesting point about this design was that the stroke of the cylinder was carefully controlled, so that if a full cartridge, with bullet, were in the cylinder, it would

15. The .450 'Pistol, Tranter, B.L., Revolver, Interchangeable' (otherwise known as 'Mark I', was introduced to the British Army in July 1878 and served until displaced by the Webley ten years later.

16, 17. The .476 'Pistol, Enfield, B.L., Revolver, Mark I', adopted by the British Army in 1880, had a short and somewhat chequered career before being replaced by the Webley. Note the peculiar extracting system, which relied on the cases being held on the extractor plate when the cylinder was pulled forward by the tipping barrel. This system was efficient enough, though the lowermost case could often be removed only by revolving the cylinder.

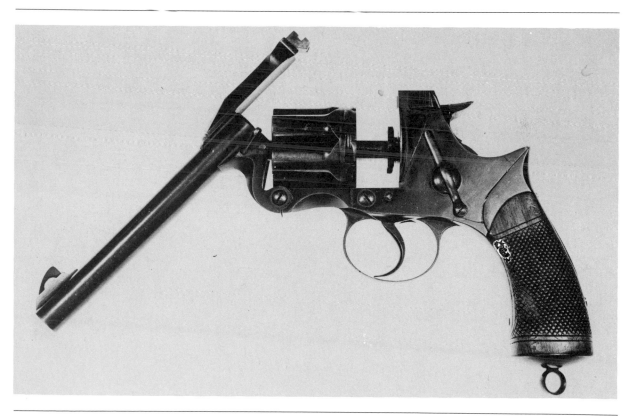

not fall clear when the gun was opened; only empty cases were short enough to come cleanly out of the chambers and fall free.

Other odd features of the Enfield design included rifling in the front end of the chambers, to give the bullet a good start, and nickel-plating of the individual pieces of the trigger and lock mechanism, the aim being to preserve them from corrosion on active service. Unfortunately, experience soon showed that these two novelties were undesirable; the chamber rifling quickly choked with fragments of lead, making it difficult to load the chambers, and the nickel plating peeled off the parts of the lock and jammed it. Both features were removed soon after production got under way.

In service it functioned well enough, but complaints about its lack of accuracy were common and in 1882 the Mark II design appeared; this had the front end of the cylinders taper-bored in an endeavour to improve accuracy, but the fact of the matter was that the standard cartridge was the .476 Eley, a design which was not particularly accurate in any pistol, though it

took some time for this to be appreciated. In any event, the Enfield stayed in service until the 1890s, but before then it had begun to be replaced by the pistol which was to be to the British Empire what the Colt was to the American West – the Webley.

Joseph and Philip Webley, of Birmingham, had been making percussion pistols since the 1850s, and when Colonel Colt's London factory closed they were able to develop a good business in quality mass-produced revolvers. In 1867 they developed their first cartridge model, which was soon adopted by the Royal Irish Constabulary and consequently became known as the 'RIC Model'. In later years it was purchased in quantity by police and military forces throughout the world, and can fairly be considered as the cornerstone of the Webley business. A solid-frame, double-action revolver in .442 calibre, it featured gate loading and rod ejection, but its virtue was the simplicity and robustness of the design, which ensured that it stayed in production until the middle 1880s, appearing in a variety of calibres. It was also

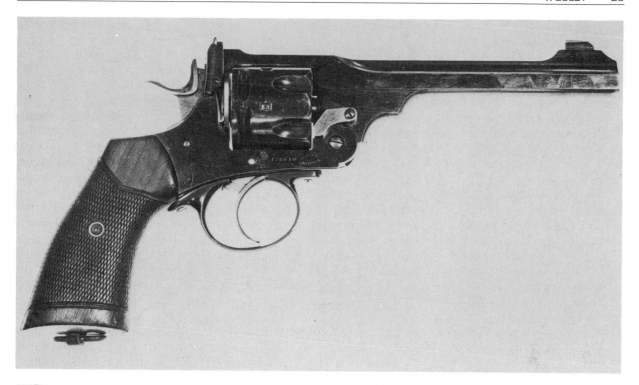

18. The .455 'Pistol, Webley, B.I., Revolver, Mark II' was adopted in 1894, though differing little fundamentally from its predecessor.

19. This .455 Webley-Wilkinson revolver, dating from c.1911, was typical of the revolvers purchased by British Army officers prior to the First World War. Virtually anything was permitted, provided it chambered the service .455 cartridge.

copied on the Continent by several makers, who generally paid the originators the compliment of calling their products 'Constabulary Revolvers'.

Webley's continued to make a number of solid-frame revolvers, but their military breakthrough came with the adoption of a hinged-frame design. This appeared first as a commercial design, but it was soon refined into the model which was ordered into production for military service in July 1887 as the Webley Mark I. It was a six-chambered, hinged-frame model, of .442 calibre, with a 4-inch barrel and double-action lock. The top strap was retained in place by the 'stirrup lock', a very solid bar which passed across the end of the top strap and was released by a thumb lever on the left side. Enormously strong, this lock kept the revolver secured against the heaviest loads and became synonymous with the Webley; it was

actually invented by a gunmaker called Edwinson Green of Cheltenham, but Webley had adopted it in 1882. This led to a somewhat acrimonious lawsuit with Green, who won, and thereafter the commercial revolvers using this lock were always called Webley-Green or 'WG' models. By the time the military contract came along, the patent was owned by Webley, and Green's name was never used in this series.

The Mark I was made in .442, .476 and .455 calibres, the Army eventually settling on .455 as their standard. Commercial revolvers were also made to the military calibre, since the British Army had an enlightened policy when it came to revolvers for officers; they could buy whatever they felt happiest with, provided it fired service ammunition, so many officers bought the more elegant Webley-Green, Webley-Wilkinson, or Army Express models, as well as less well-known designs from smaller gunmakers.

The Mark II Webley appeared in 1894; it was similar to the Mark I, but had a wider hammer spur and slightly changed stirrup lock as well as some small internal improvements which service had shown to be desirable. In 1897 the Enfield revolver was finally declared obsolete,

20. The 7.5mm Swiss Ordonnanzrevolver 1882, which drew heavily on Chamelot-Delvigne, Warnant and Schmidt predecessors, was the first smallbore revolver adopted for military service. Although the revolver was handy and well balanced, its ineffectual bullet was a poor manstopper.

and the Webley Mark III came along to replace it; this was much the same as the Mark II, but had a better cylinder rotation system and a smoother extractor. Mark IV arrived in 1899, with the result that it is often called the 'Boer War Model'. Again, the changes were relatively minor, but one notable feature is that it appeared with a number of different lengths of barrel, though the 4-inch was standard. Another significant point was that it was no longer available in .442 or .476; the Army finally had standardized on .455 and that was to remain the service calibre until the 1930s.

In April 1887 the French Army had adopted the 8mm 'Modèle 1886' Lebel rifle, using smokeless powder. It occurred to somebody that a useful amount of standardization could be achieved if the army now adopted a revolver of the same calibre, also adapted to smokeless powder. At first, as might be imagined, the reaction of the French soldiers was one of horror; the usual calibre for revolvers in military service was never less than 10mm, and preferably 12mm, in order to over-insure adequate stopping power from a slow bullet propelled by black powder. As is usual in this sort of situation, there was no shortage of scientifically minded gentlemen ready to prove to the soldiers that a small bullet moving fast had just as much terminal energy as a big bullet moving slowly. The Swiss Army had even adopted a 7.5mm revolver several years previously.

There are some flaws in this argument, since the time taken to penetrate the target and transfer the bullet's energy to it also comes into the matter, but on the face of it the argument is

persuasive and the French instructed their Saint-Etienne armoury to design a suitable revolver. Their first attempt was a solid-frame, gate-loaded weapon, issued as the 'Modèle d'Ordonnance 1887', but it was not felt to be representative of the best thinking on the subject, and after about 1,000 had been made, production stopped and the designers were sent back to their drawing-boards. The resulting weapon was the Modèle 1892, a far better weapon but, like most French designs, one with some idiosyncracies of its own.

The M1892 was a solid-frame revolver with a cylinder that swung sideways from the frame on a 'crane'; once opened, a push on the cylinder arbor rod forced out the star extractor plate to push the cartridge cases from the cylinder. This was an idea which had appeared in the USA shortly before, but the French put a new twist on it; every side-opening revolver in history has opened to the left, for the convenience of right-

21. The French 8mm Mle 1892 'Modèle d'Ordonnance' revolver, also known as the 'Lebel', was the first smallbore revolver to feature a smokeless cartridge.

22. The double-action Colt .38 Navy Revolver, introduced in 1089, was the first of a long series of similar guns. The principal weakness was the locking of the cylinder at the instant of firing; later Colts displayed bolt-notches cut around the periphery of the cylinder.

handed shooters. The M1892 is the only one which opens to the right. It also had a double-action lock, the workings of which could be inspected and cleaned by opening up the left-hand side of the frame, which is hinged at the front end so as to open like a book. On the right side is what appears to be a loading gate, but is actually the controlling catch to release the cylinder; it also locks the hammer so that it cannot move while the cylinder is opened.

The Modèle 1892 was a sound enough revolver, once one got used to its pecularities, and it was to stay in production for years and in military use until after the Second World War. But, in spite of the scientific arguments, an 8mm bullet weighing 7.7 grammes and travelling at 220 metres per second was hardly a knock-down load for a combat revolver.

The Americans had succumbed to the same argument about small calibres; made the more attractive by the indisputable fact that the .45 was something of a handful and a smaller calibre would make the pistol easier to manipulate and train on. So in 1889 the US Navy led the way by purchasing 5,000 .38 revolvers from Colt's.

In 1881, Colt's, looking for something new, had made the first solid-frame revolver with a side-swinging cylinder to a patent developed by their factory manager, William Mason. Releasing a catch allowed the cylinder to swing out on a crane, and a shaped cam automatically operated the ejector to fling the empties out without further action by the firer. This worked, but was thought to be a little too delicate for military service, so Mason redesigned it with a simpler catch and a hand-operated rod which drove out the star extractor plate. This appeared as the 1889 New Navy model, but to satisfy a US Navy demand the cylinder was made to revolve anti-clockwise, opposite to the direction usually used by Colt designs. The result was that as the ratchet-hand pushed up against the cylinder to revolve it, it also tended to force the cylinder outwards in the frame, in the direction of opening. After a while wear developed and the chamber would no longer align with the barrel, giving rise to the complaint known as 'lead-shaving' when the bullet clipped the edge of the barrel as it entered and was deformed, resulting in loss of accuracy. Nevertheless, similar models were purchased by the US Army and the US Marine Corps who used them for several years. But Colt's were not happy, even if the soldiers and sailors were, and in 1893 they redesigned the revolver, altering the mechanism to make the cylinder revolve in a clockwise direction. This was introduced to the commercial market in .32 calibre, but in 1897 they produced the New Service revolver, a heavy model capable of firing the most powerful cartridges available.

With the Webley, the Colt New Service and comparable designs from Smith & Wesson, the revolver was now in a form which most de-signers felt to be the zenith of development; in this they were not far wrong for, as we shall see later, most subsequent design has seen very little change in basic principles. Despite this degree of perfection, many inventors were convinced that they could build a better mouse-trap and seized on some fundamental aspect of the revolver and attempted to refine it.

One of the most basic defects of any revolver is that there must be a gap between the front of the cylinder and the back of the barrel; if there were no gap, the cylinder would not be free to revolve, so there is always a clearance, be it no more than a thousandth of an inch. And where there is a gap, gas from the propelling charge can escape. And if gas escapes, obviously the full effect of the cartridge is not being applied to the bullet. Moreover, as mentioned in the case of the Colt New Navy, when wear takes place a misalignment of chamber and barrel can cause lead-shaving.

There had been attempts to overcome these difficulties in the past; Collier's revolver, it will be recalled, slid the cylinder forward to enclose the rear of the barrel so as to seal in the gas. Then in 1886 a Belgian designer called Nicholas Pieper patented a system in which the essential feature was that the cartridge case had a reduced mouth which enclosed the bullet, and the weapon was so arranged that either the cylinder moved forward or the barrel moved back so that the chamber mouth enclosed the rear of the barrel and the mouth of the cartridge actually entered the rear of the bore. Thus, when the cartridge fired the mouth opened so that the metal spanned the joint between chamber and barrel, and this, together with the mating of the two parts, rendered it absolutely gas-tight. He made a few rifles, using an under-lever mechanism to force the barrel back, but for some unaccountable reason Pieper neglected to renew the patent and allowed it to lapse. And so in 1892 another Belgian, Leon Nagant, was able to come to the market with a gas-seal revolver which was very little more than a modification of the Pieper design.

Nagant was the only man who ever made a success of the gas-seal idea; he developed a solid-frame revolver which was gate loaded and rod ejecting, and arranged the mechanism so that as the pistol was cocked, the cylinder moved forward to mate with the barrel. A locking block moved in behind the cylinder, so that it did not move away from the barrel on recoil. He also developed a special cartridge in which the bullet was hidden inside the case, allowing the case to enter the barrel and provide the seal.

Nagant, some years previously, had co-operated in the design of a service rifle for the Russian Army, and this gave him the necessary connections to demonstrate his revolver to the Russians. They were contemplating a new revolver to replace the ageing Smith & Wesson .44 Russian models, and, doubtless impressed by the technical advantage and by Nagant's undoubted salesmanship, they adopted his design in 7.62mm calibre as the Model 1895 revolver. A single-action model was produced for the rank and file, and a double-action model for officers. Shortly after its adoption, the Russians began manufacture in Tula Arsenal. Russian manufacture continued into the Second World War. The revolver was an ugly beast, but, as one of the Tsar's soldiers once told me,

'If anything went wrong with the '95 you could fix it with a hammer.' The original Belgian production machinery was sold to Poland in the late 1920s, and subsequently operated in Radom for several years.

Ever since the Nagant appeared, there has been argument as to whether or not the complication of the gas seal mechanism was justified by results. It is not possible to make an exact comparative test, since there is no exactly comparable non gas-seal revolver against which one can shoot the Nagant. But experiments carried out at various times over the years suggest that the difference in muzzle velocity between a gas seal and non gas-seal revolver might amount to about 15 metres per second. The M1895 fired a 7gm bullet at 305 metres per second to give a muzzle energy of 177 Joules (240 foot-pounds). Reducing the velocity by 15

23. The 9mm Belgian Nagant revolver of 1878, a gun that inspired a host of similar designs adopted in such widely differing countries as Brazil, Sweden and Luxemburg.

m/sec brings the muzzle energy down to 160 Joules (216 ft/lb). Bearing in mind that the accepted criterion for knock-down power is 70 foot-pounds (95 Joules) there is ample power in whatever design is chosen, and there does seem to be some warrant for arguing that the Nagant design was scarcely worth the effort.

24. The Russian service Nagant of 1895. Note the long firing pin, necessary because of the forward movement of the cylinder on cocking in order to effect the gas seal.

25. The Austro-Hungarian M1898 revolver, popularly known as the 'Rast & Gasser' after its Viennese manufacturer, was a sturdy but obsolescent design. The square butt gave somewhat off-putting handling characteristics.

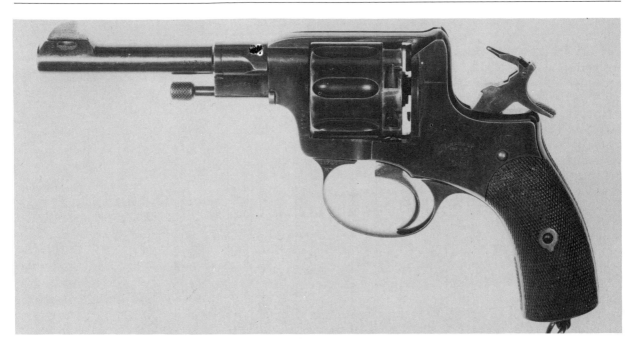

2

THE ARRIVAL OF THE AUTOMATIC PISTOL

In 1885 Maxim introduced his automatic machine-gun, which demonstrated that it was possible to produce a self-powered weapon which would reload and fire using the energy derived from the firing of the first shot. Within a very short time inventors were at work attempting to apply the same idea to hand weapons.

It would be as well at this point to stress that very few pistols can properly be called 'automatic'. The definition of an automatic weapon is quite precise: 'A weapon which, on pressure of the trigger, will fire and continue to reload and fire so long as the trigger remains pressed and the supply of ammunition is maintained.' In the early days, a number of pistols were produced which conform to this; one press of the trigger and they fired everything in the magazine in a split second. It took little time to realize that such a weapon is barely practical, since it is invariably uncontrollable as a one-hand device; the recoil simply lifts the barrel up and most of the shots spray harmlessly into the air. Fairly quickly a device called the 'disconnector' was invented, which disconnects the trigger after the first shot and will not permit another to be fired until the firer has released the trigger and re-pressed it, even though the weapon has ejected the spent case and reloaded. It is more correct, therefore, to refer to most service pistols as 'semi-automatic' or 'self-loading'. For all that, the common usage is to call them 'automatic pistols', and who are we to argue with common usage? We shall, therefore, use the term 'automatic pistol' from now on, with the proviso that when the occasional genuine full-automatic model appears it will be carefully defined as such.

The first automatic pistol to appear was a hangover from another class of weapon called (for the want of a better name) the 'mechanical repeater'. We need not dwell on these for long, since none achieved military adoption; suffice it to say that they all relied on a form of bolt action, actuated by a lever which was pushed back and forth by the firer's forefinger. In a typical repeater the firer pushed the lever forward to withdraw the bolt; he then pulled back to close the bolt and collect a cartridge from some form of magazine, feeding it into the chamber and locking the bolt behind it. Further pressure, or pressure on a separate trigger, then released a firing pin to fire the cartridge. The defect in this type of weapon is that the human forefinger is not so well adapted to deliver force in a forward direction as it is to pull, and if the weapon is dirty or the ammunition a poor fit, the physical effort required is too great.

One of these repeating pistols was the Schönberger, devised by an Austro-Hungarian inventor called Laumann. He patented this in 1890 but sold relatively few, and in 1892 he obtained a fresh patent in which the mechanism was changed to give automatic action. The breech was closed by a bolt similar to that used in a rifle, and it was held closed by a forked arm driven by a powerful spring. On firing, the cartridge attempted to blow itself out of the chamber, but the pressure of the spring and the leverage of the forked arm resisted this opening movement for just long enough to allow the bullet to leave the barrel. Thereafter the bolt, having accumulated momentum from the cartridge case's recoil, would begin to open, overcoming the resistance of the arm and spring. As it opened, so it withdrew the empty cartridge case and ejected it, and on the return stroke it collected a cartridge from a box magazine behind the chamber and loaded it.

The Schönberger (it was made at the Waffenfabrik Steyr and took its name from the factory superintendent) was in production for about a year only, and it is doubtful if more than a few dozen were made. It was in 8mm calibre, firing a rimmed cartridge which no one has ever seen, and the pistols themselves are perhaps the rarest of any handgun. It is widely believed that the Schönberger qualifies as the progenitor of all automatic pistols, though this view has recently been challenged.*

*John Walter, *The Luger Book*, pp. 22–3.

26. The 8mm Schönberger, one of the pioneering automatic pistols; the bolt has been retracted by means of the operating lever on the side.

There are three basic ways to make a self-powered automatic weapon work: by utilizing the force of recoil; by tapping the energy of the gas behind the bullet; or by using the force developed by the cartridge case in attempting to blow its way out of the chamber. One can increase the possibilities by combining these forces, or (in machine-guns) you can apply an outside power source, but we mention these possibilities only for the sake of academic completeness; they scarcely apply to pistols. The Schönberger used the last of these systems, which is described, for convenience, as the 'blowback' system, since that is precisely what the weapon does; it blows back the cartridge case so as to propel the reloading mechanism. If, as in the case of the Schönberger, some artificial restraint is placed on the movement of the breech-closing device which slows up the opening, we refer to it as 'delayed blowback'. The Schönberger had no success, but it showed that an automatic pistol was a possibility and it was not long before a more practical design made its appearance in the shape of the Borchardt pistol patented in 1893.

Hugo Borchardt was born in Germany, emigrated to America when he was 16 years old, and in about 1875 took out American citizenship. He went to work for Winchester and collaborated on the design of a number of excellent revolvers, none of which achieved production; they were used more as bargaining counters by Winchester in their commercial rivalry with Colt's. According to legend, Colt's had designed a lever-action rifle and were contemplating putting it on the market to compete with the Winchester carbine. Winchester, therefore, let it be known that they, in their turn were thinking about putting some very nice revolvers on the market. There is little doubt that Winchester would have damaged Colt's revolver sales more than Colt's would have affected Winchester's rifle sales, so the two companies agreed to stay out of each other's fields. Colt's made revolvers, Winchester made rifles, and by and large that's the way it has stayed.

Which may have made sense to Winchester and Colt but it certainly didn't please Hugo Borchardt, so in 1882 he returned to Europe and began working for the Royal Hungarian Arms Factory in Budapest. Here he saw Hiram Maxim demonstrate his machine-gun to the Austro-Hungarian Army in 1888 and was impressed by the toggle lock mechanism which Maxim used. Using his own variation of this locking system, he designed a rifle and a pistol, but there seemed to be little hope of either being adopted by the Austro-Hungarian Army and so in 1890 he travelled to Berlin and showed his designs to Ludwig Loewe. Loewe had set up in business in the 1860s making sewing-machines, but he soon realized that there was more money to be made in munitions, and by the middle 1870s was manufacturing Smith & Wesson .44 Russian pistols under Russian government contract. Loewe saw some promise in Borchardt's design, hired him, gave him the facilities he needed to complete the development, and in 1894 his pistol was put on the market.

Borchardt's pistol was built up from a butt and frame unit and a barrel and barrel extension unit, the former supporting the latter. A 'barrel extension' is simply two side arms which form part of the barrel forging, but which extend back behind the opening for the chamber. Inside this barrel extension lay the toggle unit. This consisted of a breechblock carrying a firing pin, supported by an arm hinged to a second arm, which in turn was hinged to the rear of the barrel extension. When the toggle was extended and laid flat in the extension, the breechblock closed the breech and retained the cartridge in place. On firing, the pressure on the cartridge, tending to blow it out of the chamber, was resisted by the breechblock; this was immovable, since the line of force went straight through it, through the intermediate hinge, through the rear arm and pressed on the rear hinge, so that the entire explosion pressure was contained within the barrel and barrel extension.

As a result of the projection of the bullet, the barrel unit recoiled, sliding across the top of the butt and frame. The rear arm of the toggle did not end at the rear hinge, but extended a short distance behind this pivot point. The frame of the pistol was shaped to curve up and over the rear of the barrel extension, so that as the recoiling barrel unit moved back, so this extension piece, which carried a roller, struck the curved frame. The shape of the frame caused the roller to move downwards, and in so doing it lifted the rear arm of the toggle; this 'broke' the central hinge, and the pressure in the cartridge could

now force the breechblock backwards to extract the spent case, giving the toggle a sharper bend as it did so. As soon as the toggle hinge broke, the barrel and extension stopped moving, but the breechblock continued to move back, and the movement of the rear part of the toggle was now resisted by a curved spring carried in a casing at the rear of the frame. Eventually the breechblock completed its withdrawal of the case and the spring was fully wound; the toggle stopped moving, the spring re-asserted itself, and the toggle began to fold flat once more. This drove the breechblock forward and stripped a fresh cartridge from the box magazine which was fitted into the butt of the pistol. As the toggle continued forward, so the cartridge was loaded, and eventually the toggle came to rest once more, lying flat in the barrel extension, with the barrel and extension back at the front end of the frame ready for the next shot. The firing pin had been cocked during the forward movement of the breechblock.

In the years which have passed since the Borchardt pistol first appeared, it has become normal for critics to 'knock' the design; awkward, delicate, sensitive to its ammunition, difficult to keep in working order. All this is true enough, seen with the benefit of hindsight, but in 1894 the design was a considerable achievement; bear in mind that Borchardt was working in an unknown field and had nothing to guide him except his own ingenuity and, to some extent, his knowledge of Maxim's machine-gun. Given that he was set upon using the toggle lock, it is difficult to argue with his eventual design And, it should be remembered, he had also to develop (with the assistance of the Deutsche Metallpatronenfabrik cartridge company) a rimless cartridge that could withstand the sudden accelerations and shocks of feeding in an automatic weapon. He also invented the principle of placing a removable box magazine inside the pistol butt, and he had the inspiration to make a removable wooden butt-stock which could be clipped to the rear of the frame, so turning the long-barrelled pistol into a passable carbine. The calibre was 7.65mm, the barrel was 165mm long, and the magazine held eight cartridges which it fired at a velocity of about 1,300 feet per second, which, for 1894, was real performance from a handgun.

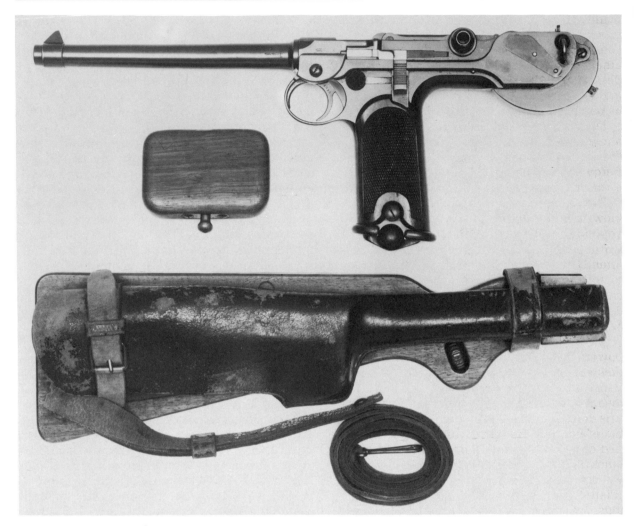

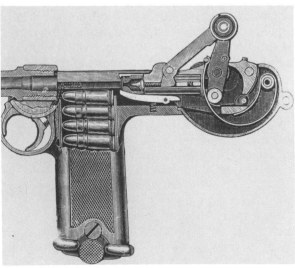

27, 28. The 7.65mm Borchardt pistol; rather more elegant than the Schönberger, but still something of a handful. The drawing shows the general construction and the unique roller-controlled toggle action.

The Loewe company made about 800 Borchardt pistols between 1894 and 1896, and these rare models can be identified by the engraving 'Waffenfabrik Loewe' on the barrel and 'System Borchardt Patent' on the frame. In 1896 Loewe reorganized his affairs and founded the Deutsche Waffen- und Munitionsfabrik (DWM); thereafter, another 2,200 or so were assembled from existing parts. These had the full DWM name on the frame.

A total of 3,000 pistols in six years may not be much by today's standards, but the Borchardt made a considerable impact; it had proved that a workable and efficient self-loading pistol could be manufactured and sold, and several other manufacturers now turned to their designers and told them to get busy. In fact, one maker had seen the light at much the same time as Borchardt and got a working automatic pistol of much simpler design on to the market within a few months of the Borchardt model. This was the comparatively unsuccessful 'Old Model' Bergmann of 1894, which was the forerunner of a variety of Bergmann designs.

The early Bergmann pistols were simple blow-back models and did not achieve military adoption, so we must ignore them, though it is worth recording that they were the first pistols intended to be simple, cheap and effective and to try and gain sales from the contemporary cheap revolvers. It was for this reason that Bergmann (or rather Schmeisser, for he was the designer) opted for the blowback system.

Military service, however, demanded a powerful weapon, since the object was to knock down an opponent as easily as with the conventional heavy-calibre revolver of the day. This meant the adoption of a locked breech, such as was done with the Borchardt, to ensure that the bullet had left the barrel and the gas pressure had dropped to a safe limit before the breech-block began to open. Delayed blowback – as we saw in the Schönberger – was not considered to be sufficiently safe for heavy loadings; it had to be a locked breech.

The man who had most experience of military requirements in Germany was, of course, Mauser. His rifles were selling all over the world but he had failed to interest any army in his Zig-Zag revolver, so when the Borchardt pistol appeared, Mauser decided to explore this avenue. As luck would have it, his factory manager, Herr Feederle had, with his two brothers, been working quietly away at an automatic pistol design for some time, and with Mauser's encouragement this now became a formal factory project. The first prototype was ready in March 1895, patents were obtained in December 1895, and the Borchardt was faced with a serious competitor.

From the engineering point of view, the Mauser was a much more elegant design than the Borchardt. In later years Borchardt expressed the view that Mauser had an easy task since

Borchardt had done all the hard work in developing the cartridge and pistol which Mauser could then examine and analyze for weaknesses. There may have been some truth in this, but there was also a fair amount of sour grapes; the Feederle brothers may even have been working on their design before the Borchardt pistol was unveiled, though it is true that Mauser took the 7.63mm Borchardt cartridge and had the design built around it. However, he made some very slight dimensional changes and loaded it with a more powerful charge; called the 7.63mm Mauser, it has become one of the immortals, still widely used today.

Mauser's pistol was similar to Borchardt's in that he used a barrel and barrel extension moving on top of a butt and frame unit, but the resemblance stopped there. The barrel extension was a square-section tunnel behind the barrel, with apertures for loading and ejection, and inside this ran the square-section bolt. This was hollow and had a firing pin inside, together with a return spring, all held together by a crossbar pushed through the barrel extension. Two ears at the rear of the bolt allowed it to be pulled back; this cocked the external hammer, and releasing the bolt allowed it to run forward and collect a cartridge from the box magazine which was a fixed unit ahead of the trigger. To load the magazine it was necessary to pull back the bolt; it stayed to the rear since the magazine platform rose and prevented forward movement. A clip of cartridges was then fitted into a slot in the barrel extension and the cartridges were swept from the clip and into the magazine by thumb pressure. As the clip was removed, so the bolt ran forward to chamber the first round.

As the bolt went forward, so did the barrel and barrel extension. Pinned underneath the barrel extension was a heavy steel block with two lugs. As the extension moved forward, this block was pulled up on to a ramp built in the frame, so that the two lugs entered two slots in the underside of the bolt. The locking block could not move down, being supported by the frame ramp, so that the bolt could not possibly move away from the breech unless the barrel and barrel extension were moved.

On firing, the whole barrel unit recoiled. As it did so, the locking block was pushed back over the frame ramp until it was able to fall free and

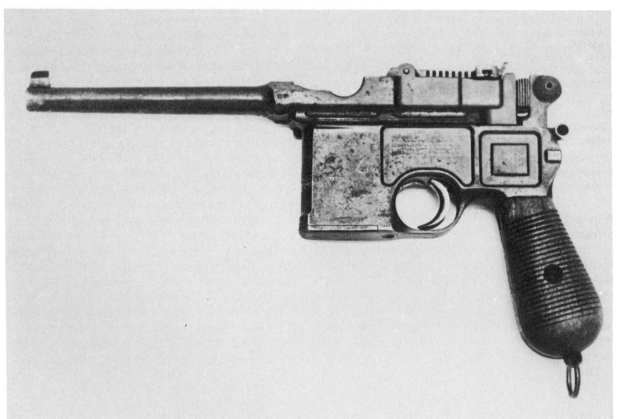

29. Dating from 1900, this six-shot 'flatside' C/96 has a unique frame forging with a shaped grip rather than the standard broomhandle pattern. Normally known as 'Officers' Models' – for no good reason – they are probably military experimentals, none of the known specimens bearing commercial proof marks.

30. This commercially proved 7.63mm 'cone hammer' Mauser C/96 pistol dates from 1899. Note the milling of the frame panels compared to the previous illustration, and the optimistic tangent-leaf back sight graduated to 1,000 metres.

31. A Mauser C/96 pistol in its wooden holster-stock, carried in a leather belt holster, with cleaning rod and spares. You have to be keen to carry this lot on your belt!

thus withdraw the lugs from the bolt. This took a fraction of a second, but it was long enough for the bullet to have left the barrel and the chamber pressure to have dropped to a safe level. Once the locking block had freed the bolt, the barrel movement stopped, the bolt flew back, cocked the hammer, returned, loaded the next round, and then the barrel ran forward again dragging the locking block across the ramp and so locking the bolt.

This all sounds very complicated, but is, in fact, one of the simplest mechanisms ever devised. It is immensely strong – no Mauser has ever been known to fail – and utterly reliable. However, it does require some very precise machining and assembly, and for this reason it is too expensive a system to be produced today. The Mauser design is also unique in that there is not a single screw or pin in the whole of the firing mechanism; it all fits together like a jigsaw and everything is retained in place by being contained inside the pistol frame.

This, then, was the Mauser C/96 – sometimes called the 'Military Model'. The earliest prototypes were based on the same mechanism, but differed in various details until the final perfected C/96 came along – C/96 stands for 'Construction of 1896'. This model, which was to be produced for many years in a number of sub-varieties, originally had a 133mm barrel and a 10-shot magazine. A few were made with a 120mm barrel and 6-shot magazine, but these failed to sell well, and Mauser smartly abandoned them. An interesting point is that the early hammer had a very large ring head so that when it was in the 'fired' position – i.e., not cocked – the curve of the ring obscured the sighting notch, a visual indication to the firer that he had forgotten to cock the pistol.

Although the Mauser pistol was an immediate success in the commercial marketplace, it aroused less interest with the military. Mauser, therefore, made a few changes: in 1898 he produced a design with a 140mm barrel, a smaller hammer head and a fully adjustable backsight graduated to 700 metres, and a wooden butt-cum-holster unit which could be clipped to the butt of the pistol to turn it into a carbine. This may have had some effect; in any event, during the early years of the twentieth century a number of armies purchased the Mauser pistol, but never in large numbers and never as their standard weapon. Turkey, China, Persia and the Italian Navy bought them, but these sales were small compared to the immense commercial sales of the Mauser. Formal military acceptance always evaded the Mauser Military, even though officers in armies throughout the world purchased and carried them; even Winston Churchill obtained one for his service in the Sudan.

The next significant design to appear was the Schwarzlose 'Standard' pistol, designed by Andreas Schwarzlose. He was, at this time, relatively unheard-of, though in later years his heavy machine-gun was to be used by the Austro-Hungarian Army. He designed his first automatic pistol in 1892, though it was never built; another abortive design in 1895, and finally the 'Standard' in 1898, and with this he achieved some degree of success. It was, potentially, a far better weapon than either the Mauser or the Borchardt, but, unfortunately, Schwarzlose came third in the race, and that, combined with some minor deficiencies in his design, meant that he never achieved the sales that he had hoped for.

The 'Standard' was an elegant-looking pistol, with a round receiver and thin, tapering barrel over a grip which was well-raked and certainly a far better ergonomic design than anything seen before. The bolt was contained in the receiver – which can be thought of as a tubular barrel extension – and it was locked into the breech by interrupted lugs which were thrust into the breech and then the bolt turned through 45° to engage the lugs. On firing, the whole unit recoiled over the frame, and a pin on the frame engaged with a curved groove in the bolt which caused the bolt to turn, and so unlock, after which the barrel stopped moving and the residual pressure and momentum of the bolt carried it back against a spring. It then

32. The Schwarzlose 'Standart', though an elegant piece of engineering, failed to make an impression on sales of the Mauser.

rebounded, taking a fresh cartridge from the butt magazine and loading it into the chamber, cocking a firing pin in the bolt as it closed.

There were minor drawbacks: the extractor, for example, did not move forward to grip the rim of the cartridge case until the firing pin went forward, which made it a trifle difficult to unload the chamber without firing the weapon. But for all that it was a good design which, with a little post-production modification, could have become one of the world's best pistols. But fate had something peculiar in store for this weapon. It sold poorly, since the Mauser was there first, and a Berlin wholesaler, who had bought the entire stock, was despairing of ever getting rid of them. Then, in 1905, some Russian revolutionaries, seeking weapons for their next coup, bought his entire stock of Schwarzlose pistols – probably about a thousand – and set about smuggling them to their comrades in Russia. 'Acting upon information received' no doubt, the Tsar's police got to know of the plot and seized the entire shipment, after which, rather than look a gift horse in the mouth, the pistols were issued to police and customs guards. And because of that almost the entire production of Schwarzlose pistols finished up in Russia, and they are extremely uncommon outside that country.

There were now three locked-breech pistols on the market, and yet the military procurement officers, after testing them, made no moves towards adopting them for service. The principal reason was that while they were all masterly designs, they were designs which had been developed by pure technicians, concerned with making the weapon work and concerned with solving engineering problems. They had not been designed by men conversant with the realities of warfare; all three were long-barrelled, temperamental unless carefully maintained, expensive and not well-suited to quick manipulation in the heat of close combat. One man saw this defect and set about rectifying it.

Georg Luger was a doctor's son, had served in the Austro-Hungarian Landwehr for four years, then left at the age of 23 to marry and go into engineering. His military service had taught him something about the practical use of firearms, and in 1875 he met Count Ferdinand von Mannlicher, a famous weapons designer, and collaborated with him in the development of a rifle magazine. Although Luger was now a professional railway engineer, this brief exposure to weapons technology appears to have roused some hidden talent, and he began designing rifles of various sorts. In 1891 he went to Berlin and joined the Loewe company as a consultant designer.

Loewe, it seems, was not happy at the slow sales of the Borchardt pistol and with the way that the Mauser was gaining the ascendancy, and he asked Borchardt to overhaul his design. Borchardt, like many gifted designers, had put the thing behind him once it had gone into production, and was thinking about fresh ideas, notably an automatic rifle. Nevertheless, he appears to have tinkered with the pistol to try and improve it, though one is left with the feeling that he felt it was a masterpiece as it stood and that tinkering with it would be unlikely to improve anything. Luger appears to have collaborated with Borchardt on the first changes and also made an important change in the ammunition, but it is almost certain that in about 1896 Borchardt had had enough and left it to Luger to make what he could of the pistol. Luger had a pretty good idea of what was wanted in a military weapon and he was single-minded enough to stick at it until he had perfected his ideas into a working model.

The first sign of change came with the submission of a pistol officially known as the 'Borchardt-Luger' for trials by the Swiss Army in 1898. It was scarcely recognizable as the same weapon that had appeared four years before. Gone was the awkward, bulbous overhang behind the grip, gone was the equally awkward upright grip, which had been replaced on an experimental Borchardt-like pistol by a grip which sloped back at 55° to the frame so that the pistol instinctively pointed towards its target when gripped naturally. The curved return spring was now replaced by a flat leaf spring in the rear of the grip, connected to the toggle by a bell-crank, and the toggle broke by having the central hinge strike a ramp cut in the rear of the frame. Though retaining some Borchardt-like features, the trigger mechanism was improved, and a grip safety device was let into the rear surface of the butt; unless the pistol were correctly held, the trigger could not be pressed and it would not fire.

The pistol did well in its trials, but the Swiss suggested some small improvements. They asked for a manual safety catch to be fitted to the frame, feeling that the grip safety was insufficient to guarantee complete safety; there were small changes in the frame contour and the breechblock which made the action smoother. Unlike the earlier submissions from DWM, the new Borchardt-Luger chambered what has since become known as the 7.65mm Parabellum cartridge, the word 'Parabellum' being the telegraphic address of the DWM Company's head office in Berlin. Shortening the cartridge reduced the recoil, making the pistol more controllable and more accurate, and it also allowed the whole mechanism to be made more compact since the breechblock made a

33. Luger improved the Borchardt by changing the clock spring to a neater spring (originally a riband, but later a coil) in the grip behind the magazine well. The toggle-lock concept was retained, though the entire gun was tidied up.

34. The German Navy's Parabellum, the Selbstladepistole 1904, had a distinctive 15cm barrel and a two-position sliding back sight on top of the toggle.

shorter stroke. With all these improvements incorporated the pistol was now re-submitted to the Swiss in 1899; it was approved and on 4 May 1900 they formally adopted the 'Pistol, Ordonnanz 1900, System Borchardt-Luger'. It was the first automatic pistol to achieve full military adoption.

It will be recalled that Luger's mentor in his youth had been Count von Mannlicher; he was a prolific designer of firearms, and had done a great deal of experimenting with automatic rifles in the early 1890s, but the automatic rifle was, at that time, something from which the military shied away. Give the soldiers automatic rifles, they said, and they'll blaze away all their ammunition in the first two minutes of the battle and then sit still to be bayoneted or shot. Time has proved them wrong, of course, but that was their attitude in the late nineteenth century – and it also extended to machine-guns and quick-firing artillery to a greater or lesser extent. There was rather less worry over automatic pistols since in most armies these would be confined to officers and NCOs who, it was

assumed, were better disciplined; moreover, they would never have very much ammunition – generally one full magazine and sufficient rounds to refill it once or perhaps twice. This was because the carriers of pistols were not expected to get into situations where they needed much ammunition; they were usually leaders who would be more concerned with giving orders and chasing their men around. If they needed a pistol, it would be a last-ditch effort and a superfluity of ammunition wouldn't help them much.

Mannlicher, therefore, began to look at the possibility that an automatic pistol might be more attractive to his military customers (who bought his bolt-action magazine rifles in vast quantities). After one or two aberrant early designs, in 1896 he produced a military pistol which, since he didn't bother to put it into pro-

35. The German Army 'artillery' Parabellum, the Lange Pistole 08, was adopted in 1913. The 20cm barrel and tangent-leaf back sight were intended to be used in conjunction with a board-type shoulder-stock to improve long-range shooting.

duction for some years, has come to be known as his 1903 Model. It resembled the Mauser in having a fixed box magazine ahead of the trigger and a similar barrel, barrel extension and bolt, but the locking system for the bolt was much simpler. It consisted of a strut which hinged up from the rear of the barrel extension to wedge itself behind the bolt, forced there by a block on the frame. Not only was it simpler, it was also rather weaker than the Mauser system, and this proved to be the pistol's downfall. Mannlicher had developed his own cartridge for the Model 1903, a 7.65mm bottle-necked round which was dimensionally the same as the Borchardt or Mauser cartridges but loaded for a lower velocity. So long as the Mannlicher cartridge was fired in the Mannlicher pistol, all was well; but, of course, the inevitable happened and people began firing Mauser cartridges out of it, in order to get a little bit more performance, and the locking system failed to stand up to much of that treatment. This did the Mannlicher's reputation no good at all; it was entered for trials in Switzerland in 1898 but failed to impress the testers.

Mannlicher decided he had been too complicated, so in 1898 he patented a fresh design which eventually appeared as his Model 1901. This was perhaps the most graceful automatic pistol ever made; it balances perfectly in the hand, is accurate, has a light recoil, and generally is everything you would wish for – except in stopping power. It was a delayed blowback design, using a breechblock which had arms reaching forward, around the lower part of the fixed barrel and frame, so as to enclose a return spring. There was an external hammer, cocked by the recoiling block, and the opening of the breech was slightly delayed by a leaf spring alongside the block which pressed up to add friction during the opening movement. The magazine was a box inside the butt, but it was not removable; like the Mauser and earlier Mannlicher, it had to be loaded from a clip, after the breechblock had been pulled back.

36. The 1901-model Mannlicher pistol was a graceful blowback, but achieved only limited success despite being adopted as the service pistol of Argentina in 1905. The gun illustrated is marked Md.1905 and WAFFENFABRIK STEYR on the left side of the frame above the grip.

One slight drawback to this type of weapon is that once the rounds are in the magazine it requires some special mechanism to get them out again without firing or without having to work the slide or breech mechanism back and forth to eject them one by one. The Mannlicher has a catch at the top of the magazine which can be depressed; this releases the entire contents so that they are driven out of the open action by the magazine spring. And unless you are quick off the mark with something to catch them, they usually erupt into the air and fall into the nearest patch of mud.

The Model 1901 sold moderately well on the commercial market and it was widely purchased by officers of the German and Austro-Hungarian armies. It failed to get adopted by any European army, largely because it did not have a locked breech, but a number of South American armies bought it, notably the Argentine Army, and its special 7.65mm straight-sided Mannlicher cartridge is still manufactured in Argentina.

It will be seen that 7.65mm had become more or less the standard for military pistols, princi-pally because every designer was saving himself extra work by taking the Borchardt cart-ridge as his model. But many armies were far from convinced that this calibre was satisfactory as a combat bullet; they were accustomed to heavy lead bullets and they were suspicious of these small jacketed items.

The German Army was one of these doubters. Towards the end of the nineteenth century major trials had been undertaken with the Mauser C/96, but the Mauser had proved less than reliable and many of the testers – though they were impressed with the high velocity of the bullet – were sceptical about the small calibre. When the Borchardt-Luger appeared, it, too, offered a 7.65mm bullet. Although the pistol was impressively reliable, the authorities sought a harder-hitting weapon. Consequently, Luger simply opened out the mouth of the 7.65mm Parabellum round so that it was straight-sided and would accept a 9mm calibre bullet. His first attempt was, in fact, still slightly

37. A longitudinal section of the 1896-patent Mannlicher, a Mauser C/96 lookalike, resurrected in 1903 without conspicuous success.

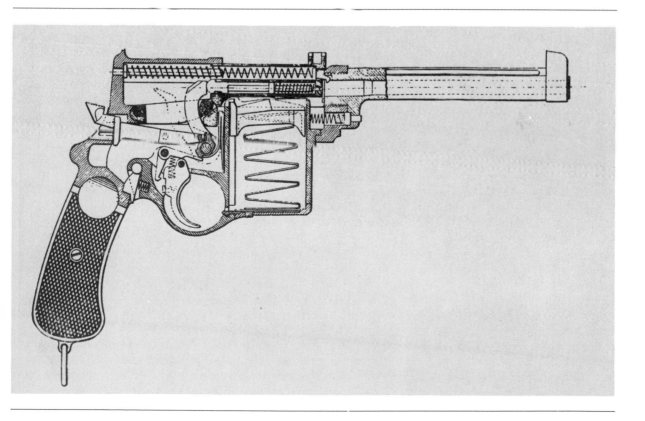

bottle-necked, but he soon discarded this and by 1903 had the first of what was to become famous as the '9mm Parabellum' cartridge. In an endeavour to improve the stopping power of the bullet, it had a conical nose and a flattened tip.

Trials of modified Borchardt-Luger or 'Parabellum' pistols continued throughout 1903–4 until the army experts were satisfied that the gun was combatworthy. During this period, the German Navy decided to adopt a new pistol; however, it was accepted that the Parabellum would ultimately be adopted by the army and the experiments were simply to find the best type of Parabellum. By this time, and on the verge of large-scale enlargement, the navy was desperately short of handguns and it seems that an 'interim' pistol – with a leaf-type mainspring – was rushed into production while DWM readied the perfected 'new pattern' gun with a coil spring and a simplified toggle without the rebound suppressor. Luger had previously perpetuated the 'anti-bounce lock' that had been a feature of Borchardt's toggle.

This mechanism is believed to have been due to Borchardt's experience with rifles; with automatic rifles and light machine-guns there is a distinct possibility that the breechblock, after closing behind the cartridge with some force, may bounce open again before the firing pin has reached the cartridge cap. This means that when the weapon fires, the cartridge may well be slightly out of the chamber and the breech improperly locked. To prevent this it was usual to incorporate some form of lock which prevented the breech bouncing open.

On the Borchardt and the early Borchardt-Lugers, this takes the form of a clip on the right side of the toggle which engages with a specially cut rib on the frame. As the toggle reaches the end of the closing stroke, the clip engages with the rail so that upward movement of the toggle is impossible. It also means that when cocking the pistol, by pulling on the two knobs on the toggle hinge, it is necessary to draw the toggle unit straight back for a short distance, to disconnect the anti-bounce lock, before lifting it to break the toggle and open the breech. As it happens, the Borchardt toggle is one mechanism which doesn't need an anti-bounce lock; when the toggle closes, it does not, in fact, lie flat, but actually passes over-centre so that

there is a slight downward bend in the toggle hinge. If, therefore, the breech attempts to open, the movement of the toggle will be downward and the frame will resist it. Consequently, bounce is impossible. Luger eventually realized and dispensed with the lock.

None of the perfected navy guns were delivered until early 1906, by which time perhaps 1,500 of the interim model had been delivered. The various subvarieties of the navy Luger were all known officially as 'Selbstladepistole 1904', with 15cm barrels, a safety catch that moved up to lock the grip mechanism and 6-groove rifling. By the time the finalized navy pistol appeared, the army had also decided to take the Parabellum; however, Mauser managed to defer the decision while his new pistols were tested (unsuccessfully, as things transpired) and the commitment of the funds to rearming with Mauser rifles prevented the army Parabellum being adopted until 22 August 1908, even though small numbers of commercial-type New Model Parabellums had been acquired for machine-gun units in 1906–7. General issue commenced in 1909, and the 'Pistole 1908' remained regulation issue until 1945 – by which time something in the region of three million Parabellums had been made in a variety of shapes and sizes.

The German Army was not the first of the pre-1914 'major powers' to adopt an automatic pistol for general army issue; this honour fell to the Austro-Hungarian Army which just beat the Germans with the Roth-Steyr pistol. This was a very odd weapon indeed, and was the product of two original thinkers, Georg Roth and Karel Krnka. Roth was primarily a cartridge manufacturer with factories in Vienna and Pressburg (which is now Bratislava in Czechoslovakia), while Krnka was a weapons designer who had some useful rifle inventions to his credit. Krnka became Roth's factory manager in 1898 and thereafter the two collaborated on several pistol designs; manufacture was by the Austrian Weapons Factory at Steyr, from which came the name Roth-Steyr.

The Roth-Steyr Model 1907, which was adopted by the Austro-Hungarian Army for issue to cavalry troops, used an entirely new method of locking the breech closed during firing. The most remarkable item is the bolt, which extends for the full length of the receiver;

the forward portion of this bolt is hollow, and when the bolt is closed this section completely surrounds the barrel, the rear end being solid except for a hole for the firing pin. The bolt fits inside the tubular receiver – the body of the pistol – which is forged and forms part of the pistol frame. The barrel has four lugs: two near the breech which fit into two grooves cut into the interior of the bolt's hollow section, and two near the muzzle which fit into curved grooves cut into the muzzle bush.

On firing, the bolt is locked to the barrel by the rear barrel cams being engaged in the grooves in the bolt, so the two recoil together. As the barrel is thus pulled through the muzzle bush, the two lugs run in the cam grooves and rotate the barrel through 90°. This pulls the rear lugs around until they disengage from their locked position and align with that part of the grooves which are cut in a straight line; this therefore unlocks the bolt which is now free to continue back while the barrel stops due to the front lugs meeting the end of their grooves. The

empty case is ejected from a slot in the bolt, a return spring is compressed, and when the bolt reaches the end of its travel it starts back towards the chamber. It collects a fresh round from the integral butt magazine and loads it into the chamber; the pressure of the spring then pushes the barrel forward so that the muzzle bush grooves rotate it and the rear lugs move into the locking section of the bolt grooves. It is a strong and reliable mechanism but, as can be imagined, one which demands exquisite manufacture and careful fitting; one hesitates to think what it would cost to make such a pistol today.

The other interesting feature of the Roth-Steyr is the firing mechanism. It was, you will recall, intended for use by the cavalry, and it seems probable that they expressed some doubt about pistols with the usual sort of single-action trigger and hammer, especially if the horse

38. The Roth-Steyr, or Repetierpistole M7, was issued to Austro-Hungarian cavalrymen.

39. The 'Steyr-Hahn' pistol, a commercial adaptation of the Roth-Steyr adopted by the Austro-Hungarians for service during the First World War. This is a wartime gun, evident from the date.

were a bit restless. So when the Roth-Steyr has reloaded itself, the firing pin is not cocked; it requires a long pull on the trigger to fire, and this movement first cocks the firing pin and then releases it. In order to fire the Roth-Steyr you have to mean it; accidental discharge is virtually impossible. It looks a somewhat cumbersome weapon, but it actually handles quite well, once you get used to the trigger pull. It fires a special 8mm cartridge which is still manufactured in Italy. The gun stayed in production until the late 1920s and large numbers of them turned up in the Balkans during the Second World War, and probably are still around in some numbers in that area.

Georg Roth died in 1909 and Krnka moved to the Hirtenberger Patronenfabrik (Cartridge Factory) in Austria. He continued to design pistols for other people, and his next design was adopted by the Austro-Hungarian Army for their infantry in 1914. It was manufactured at Steyr, initially for commercial sale as the Steyr 1911, and it used a very powerful 9mm cart-

ridge also known by the Steyr name. The Model 1911 looks rather more 'ordinary' than the Roth-Steyr of 1907, but the basic principle of operation is the same – a rotating barrel. There is a slide, moving on top of the pistol frame and carrying the barrel. The rear of the slide forms the breechblock and contains a firing pin, and there is a conventional external hammer; the unofficial name for this in Austria was the 'Steyr-Hahn' (Steyr with hammer) to distinguish it from the earlier non-hammer design. Two lugs on top of the barrel engage in slots cut in the slide, and one lug beneath the barrel engages in a helical groove cut in the frame. When the hammer is released, it strikes the firing pin and the cartridge is fired. The barrel and slide are locked together by the two lugs, so both recoil together. As the barrel moves, so its bottom lug rides in the curved groove in the frame and the barrel is rotated, though only through a distance of about 20°. This, as before, turns the top lugs out of the locking slots and aligns them with a straight slot in the slide. The barrel stops when the bottom lug reaches the end of its groove, but the slide is now unlocked and free to continue its recoil stroke to eject and reload, cocking the hammer as it goes back.

As with all Krnka's designs, the magazine is integral in the butt and loaded by pulling back the slide and putting in a charger of ten cartridges, sweeping the cartridges out of the charger and into the magazine with the thumb. The mechanism is strong and simple, and the gun is most reliable; with its original cartridge it is something of a handful, but when the Austrian Army was integrated into the German Army in 1938 many of these pistols were modified to fire the German standard 9mm Parabellum cartridge, and with this round the Steyr 1911 is a very nice pistol indeed. As well as being used by the Austro-Hungarian and (later) Austrian Armies, the Model 1911 was also used by the Roumanian and Chilean forces and by the Bavarian Army during the First World War. Manufacture ceased in 1918 and was never resumed, but one is inclined to

wonder whether it might not have had greater success had it been chambered for a more easily obtainable cartridge in the first place.

One final Continental design to be considered is the locked-breech pistol which Bergmann finally got around to designing. As we have already said, he had begun his pistol business by producing a number of blowback weapons for the commercial market, and although he often put these up for military test they were always rejected. In 1901 he had designed a machine-gun which used a vertically moving block of steel to lock the breech, and later in that year he adapted this method to a pistol mechanism. His 1897-vintage 'Bergmann No. 5' model had resembled the Mauser in having a fixed box magazine ahead of the trigger and a breech bolt offset laterally into the receiver wall. However, the No. 5 failed to make any headway. It was replaced by the Bergmann 'Mars', based on the contemporary Bergmann machine-gun, which featured a

40. The Bergmann-Bayard, made in Belgium, was adopted by Spain, Greece and Denmark – in the latter's case, apparently because the Germans wouldn't grant a licence to make the Parabellum. This is an M.10/21, modified by the Haerens Tøjhus after the end of the First World War

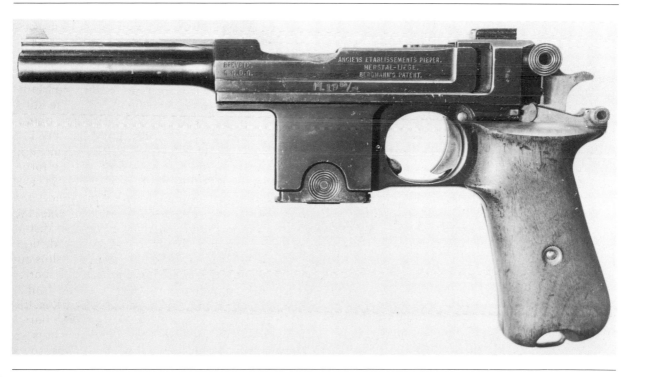

breech bolt of square section moving in a square barrel extension above the frame. As the bolt moved forward to lock, so the barrel extension pulled along a bar of steel which rode on a ramp in the frame and moved up to enter a slot in the bottom of the bolt. Since it was located in a slot in the bottom of the barrel extension, it thus locked the bolt to the barrel very securely, which was just as well since Bergmann chose to use a very powerful 9mm cartridge of his own design; it is, in fact, almost identical with the 9mm Steyr in size and power.

Bergmann marketed this as the 'Mars' pistol, and in 1905 the Spanish Army tested it, found it satisfactory, and decided to adopt it. Bergmann had at last got his wish, a nice fat military contract, but at the moment of his triumph things fell apart. His own factory was really little more than a large warehouse, and he had always had his pistols produced by another company, the V. C. Schilling factory at Suhl in Germany. Shortly after Bergmann got his Spanish contract and had supplied a few hundred pistols, Schilling were bought out by another company, Heinrich Krieghoff, and

41. The Webley-Fosbery automatic revolver, showing the actuating tracks cut in the surface of the cylinder. These revolved the cylinder partly during recoil and partly during run-out.

Krieghoff cancelled the agreement whereby the factory made Bergmann's pistols. So there stood Bergmann with a contract but no means of fulfilling it. Rather than suffer any further distress he chose to get out of the pistol business entirely, and he sold the patents and the contract to a Belgian company, the Ancien Etablissments Pieper of Herstal, near Liège. They produced the Spanish order and then went on to market the pistol, with some minor changes, as the 'Bergmann-Bayard' ('Bayard' being their trademark) on the commercial market. They also sold it to the Danish government; production continued at the Haerens Tøjhus (Copenhagen) after the end of the First World War, and the Danish forces were equipped with it until after 1945.

Turning now to England, we find that the automatic pistol was having a hard time to gain acceptance. Numbers of the Continental designs were on sale, but they were expensive

42. Loading the Webley-Fosbery, with a Prideaux quick-loading device.

compared to a revolver and because of their small calibre they could make no progress towards military acceptance. The first essay into automatic operation came with the adaptation of a revolver design.

Colonel George Vincent Fosbery, VC, had been interested in firearms throughout his life, patenting breech-loading cartridges and a rifle as early as 1866. In 1895 he took out a patent for a self-loading revolver, based on the Colt Model 1873 design; this aroused the interest of the Webley company and between them they eventually developed the Webley-Fosbery automatic revolver, the first of which appeared in 1901.

The Webley-Fosbery was basically a service pattern Webley revolver divided into two. The butt and frame constituted one unit, and on these the barrel and cylinder were fitted so that they could slide back and forth. The cylinder had a zigzag groove cut on its outer surface and this engaged with a fixed pin in the frame. The barrel hinged downwards to open, in the usual way, and the cylinder was loaded with six .455 cartridges. The barrel was closed again and the pistol was cocked by thumbing back the hammer. On firing, recoil drove the barrel unit back on the frame, and the fixed pin, riding in the grooves on the cylinder, rotated it through one-twelfth of a turn. At the same time the hammer was recocked by the movement of the barrel unit. After cocking the hammer a return spring pushed the barrel unit back to the firing position, and as it did so the fixed pin gave the cylinder another one-twelfth of a turn so that a new chamber was now aligned with the barrel and hammer.

The Webley-Fosbery was also made in an eight-chambered .38 calibre model, rarely seen today, and it was a pleasant pistol to fire since a good deal of the recoil was absorbed by the moving barrel unit. By the same token, it was necessary to hold it fairly firmly, preferably stiff-armed, since a slack hold would allow most of the recoil to be taken up by movement of the hand and arm, so that there was less to operate the mechanism. Although heavy – about six

43. An example of the 9mm Gabbett-Fairfax 'Mars'.

ounces heavier than a standard .455 Webley revolver – it proved popular and numbers of British officers purchased them, though they were never approved as a military issue weapon. They remained popular until the First World War when it was discovered that, while they worked admirably in most situations, the mud and filth of Flanders tended to jam their mechanism and make them unreliable.

While Webley were developing the Webley-Fosbery they were approached by another English inventor, Hugh Gabbet-Fairfax, with a design of automatic pistol he was anxious to produce. He was another man with a long-standing love of firearms and had obtained many patents in the 1890s, one of which concerned a most complicated pistol. He produced a prototype in 1897 and offered it to Webley, but though they were interested in finding a design to manufacture as their own, they declined to adopt the Gabbet-Fairfax model (called the 'Mars', which can be confusing in view of the Bergmann 'Mars' already mentioned) but agreed to manufacture it for him.

Gabbet-Fairfax was aiming at military acceptance; hitherto every automatic pistol put up to the British Army had been turned down because the target effect was insufficient – it failed to meet the same stringent demand, that of knocking down an enraged native tribesman, which was met by the .455 revolver bullet. The answer, thought Gabbet-Fairfax, was high velocity and, in the words of a contemporary magazine, 'He allowed his ideals to wander in the direction of high ballistics and his pistols took on the form of young cannon.' The pistol worked on a system which is relatively uncommon, that of 'long recoil'. In this system the barrel and bolt are locked together and recoil for a distance greater than the length of a complete cartridge. They then stop, the bolt is unlocked (by rotation, in the case of the Mars), and the barrel is allowed to run back to its forward position. In doing so it allows the empty case to be pulled from the chamber by the extractor on the bolt, and a mechanical ejector springs up and knocks the case clear of the gun. A mechanical lifter withdraws a cartridge backwards out of the magazine and raises it into the path of the bolt. All this takes place after the shot has been fired and while the firer is still holding the trigger back. He now releases the trigger and this releases the bolt, so that it can run forward, collect the fresh cartridge held by the lifter, thrust it into the chamber, then rotate and lock into the barrel. During the rearward stroke a massive hammer has been cocked, and thus the pistol is now ready to fire once more.

The Mars was produced in three calibres, 8.5mm, 9mm and .45, and there were a variety of cartridges of differing size and potency produced at various times to suit them. As an example, his 9mm pistol fired a 156-grain bullet at 1,650 feet per second to give a muzzle energy of 943 foot-pounds, and his .45 Long cartridge gave 1,200 feet per second and 700 foot-pounds. For seventy years the Mars was undoubtedly the most powerful automatic pistol ever made, but the price to be paid was one which no army would accept. To put it mildly, the Mars was highly unpleasant to fire, since it kicked like a mule. It was tested by the Royal Navy in 1902 and while they admitted that it gave all the stopping power anyone could want,

they added the rider that, 'No one who once fired this pistol wished to shoot with it again . . .'

It was left to Webley's own designer, W. J. Whiting, to produce the first practical British automatic pistol. His first models appeared in 1904, in very small numbers, and in 1906 a .32 calibre blowback was placed on the market, followed by .25 calibre models. These were reasonably popular, but one of Whiting's prototypes had been a locked breech pistol in .455 calibre, aimed at military adoption and in 1909, in response to requests from potential European customers who wanted a powerful pistol but not one as powerful as .455, Webley produced a 9mm model. However, the 9mm cartridge was yet another type, the 9mm Browning Long, developed in Belgium and less powerful than the 9mm Parabellum.

In 1912 the aim was achieved when the Royal Navy approved issue of the 'Pistol, Self-Loading, .455 Mark I'. This was a heavy and sub-

44. The Webley & Scott 'Pistol, Self-Loading, .455 Mark I', as issued to the Royal Navy.

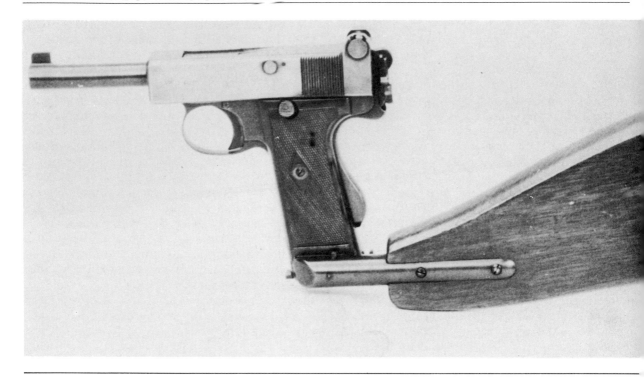

45. A rare version of the Webley & Scott pistol fitted with a shoulder-stock for use by Royal Flying Corps observers in the days before machine-guns were fitted to aircraft.

stantial weapon which used a large lug on top of its barrel to lock slide and barrel together. The slide was a boxy unit on top of the frame, while the barrel protruded from the front; on firing, the two moved back together until the barrel was moved downward by oblique lugs alongside the chamber moving in slots in the frame. As the barrel slid down, so the top lug came free from the slide, the barrel stopped, and the slide continued to the rear to eject the spent case, cock the hammer, and then return to load the chamber from the removable box magazine carried in the butt.

The Webley automatic was a robust weapon, and it fired a potent, round-nosed .455 jacketed bullet. But somehow the grace of the Webley revolvers was not carried over to the automatic pistols, and they were angular, square and ugly. The principal defect in the eyes of practical shooters was that the grip was too square to the frame; grasp a Webley naturally and you will find that the barrel is pointing at the floor fifteen yards or so away. It requires a conscious effort to bend the wrist in order to get the barrel

parallel with the ground, which is why contemporary pictures of people shooting the Webley invariably show them adopting a rather awkward stance.

The Webley had one or two good points, though: it was possible, for example, to release the magazine and lock it again out of engagement with the slide, so that it was possible to hand-load a cartridge in the breech and fire it without the returning slide reloading. In fact the slide stayed open and one could continue to hand-load individual rounds and fire; then when an emergency arose, a quick slap of the hand brought the magazine into engagement and seven shots were immediately available. This was similar to the 'cut-off' used with military magazine rifles of the period, designed to allow soldiers to fire single shots at a deliberate rate, but still have the contents of their magazine ready in case the enemy made a rush. Another plus point was the take-down: slide and barrel can be taken from the frame in less than two seconds, one of the quickest and simplest dismantling routines of any locked-breech pistol.

The Webley Mark I remained in service use until the Second World War, though it was confined to the Royal Navy, the RFC and the RAF;

Fabrique Nationale had been formed some years previously by a consortium of Liège gunmakers in order to manufacture Mauser rifles under licence for the Belgian Army. This gave them some expertise in military requirements, but the directors, being commercial gunmakers, were also astute enough to realize that there was an enormous civilian market waiting for a cheap, reliable, pocket automatic pistol. It must be appreciated that there were no laws against owning pistols anywhere in Europe at that time, and pistols for home and personal defence were commonplace. The demand was satisfied by cheap revolvers, made by the thousand in Germany, Belgium and France, but FN felt sure that an automatic pistol would soon make its mark. By 1898 they had produced a suitable design, which was based on Browning's ideas.

This first Browning pistol was a simple but clever design which used the blowback system of operation. The butt and frame supported the barrel, which locked into a forging on the frame. Around this was a slide which was slab-sided and which had the return spring fitted into a tunnel above the barrel. The rear of the slide was formed as the breechblock, and there was a hammer in the frame, concealed beneath the rear of the slide. The return spring was trapped between the front of the slide and the lug which carried the barrel, and through it passed a connecting rod which was attached to an arm hanging down from the top of the slide. This arm went into a slot in the breechblock section and engaged with the firing pin.

On firing, the slide moved backwards, pulling on the rod and thus pulling on the return spring. As the slide moved back, so the spent case was ejected. On the return stroke, pulled by the spring, the hanging arm pulled the slide back and it also pulled on the firing pin; but the forward movement of the firing pin was stopped by the trigger mechanism, so that once the slide stopped moving, with a new cartridge in the breech, it was actually the return spring which was waiting to propel the firing pin forward once the trigger was pressed. After trials in various places the pistol was adopted by the Belgian Army in 1900, in spite of the fact that it was chambered for a relatively weak 7.65mm cartridge which Browning had designed expressly for this weapon.

experience in Flanders during the First World War, when the pistol was issued to Royal Horse Artillery personnel, showed that the close-fitting machined surfaces did not function well in mud and dirt and it was soon replaced by revolvers.

We must now step back a few years and look at what had been happening in the United States of America while the automatic pistol had been making its mark in Europe. In fact, development in the USA was slow; the Americans were firmly wedded to their revolvers, and the only prominent designer who took any interest in the automatic pistol was John Browning. This is scarcely surprising since he had already developed a practical machine-gun, which was adopted by the US Army in 1895, and following this he took out a number of patents covering various blowback pistol designs. He attempted to interest the Colt company, but the only automatic they wanted to see was a heavy-calibre model suitable for military use. Browning therefore went to Belgium where he entered into an agreement with Fabrique National d'Armes de Guerre of Liège by which FN were to have the freedom to develop his patents and market the resulting weapons in the Eastern Hemisphere.

46. The FN-Browning Mle 1900 or 'Old Model'.

47. The Mle 1903 FN-Browning – shown here with its wood body holster-stock attached – was popular in military circles.

The Model 1900 enjoyed good commercial sales, but FN were not satisfied, and set about developing an even simpler design. This they produced as the Model 1903, or 'Modèle de Guerre'. In this design they reduced the automatic pistol to its simplest possible form consistent with reliability. It consisted of three major components: the barrel, the frame and the slide. The slide moved across the frame in grooves and carried a simple firing pin in its rear, breechblock, section. The barrel was fitted in place by three lugs underneath its breech end; these engaged in three grooves cut in the frame and the barrel was held down into the grooves by the interior fit of the slide over its top. To remove the barrel, all that was necessary was to pull the slide back until the muzzle was exposed, then rotate the barrel until the grooves came free, after which slide and barrel could be slid forward and off the frame. Beneath the barrel was the return spring, its front end pressing against the front inside of the slide, the rear end against the frame. Firing was performed by a hammer, concealed inside the frame, which struck the firing pin when the trigger was pressed. The calibre was 9mm, and this pistol introduced the 9mm Browning Long cartridge, which was about the same size as the Parabellum, but fired a round-nosed bullet with a much lower charge; it was designed to be as powerful as possible while still permitting the use of an unlocked breech.

The Model 1903 was an instant success. The Belgian Army adopted it in place of the Model 1900, the Swedish Army adopted it and, after FN stopped production of it, continued to manufacture it in Sweden until 1941, and still have it in service. It was made in millions, and in some parts of Europe the word 'Browning' is used to mean 'automatic pistol'. And for every one that FN made, a score were made by pirates who stole the design.

The simplicity of the Model 1903 made it attractive to manufacturers with little

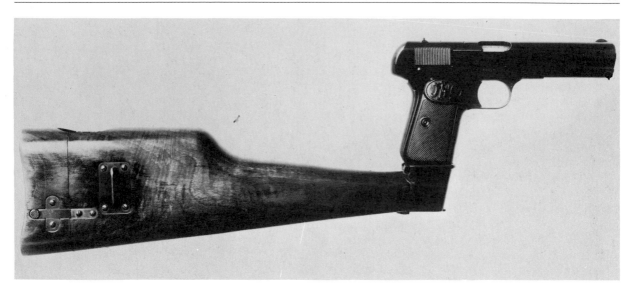

machinery, and prominent in this group were the Spanish gunmakers in Eibar, a small town in the north of Spain. Here gunmaking had been carried on for centuries and there were scores of one-man businesses scratching a living making revolvers. The simplicity of the Browning design was a gift, and they seized it with both hands. They were able to do this because of the peculiar patent laws which operated in Spain at that time. In brief, nothing which was not actually sold in Spain could be patented there, so a smart operator could, by copying a foreign design and placing it on sale, actually patent it before the unfortunate foreignor knew what was happening. By 1905 copies of the Browning 1903 model were appearing in hundreds and the volume increased until it was abruptly halted by the Civil War. The design had one or two minor alterations to suit Spanish methods of manufacture, and the calibre was more often 7.65mm than 9mm, but their parentage was never in doubt. They appeared with every conceivable name from AAA via Apache, Basque, Chanticleer, Grand Precision, Looking Glass, Lusitania, and Oscillant-Azul to Zulaica. They can be found marked in every language to suggest manufacture anywhere else but Spain, and with a fine crop of forged proof-marks. They range from the satisfactory to the downright dangerous and they form a fascinating study on their own. And yet, even with that sort of competition, FN still made Browning pistols by the million.

Once Browning had seen his blowback pistols into good hands, and doubtless once he had begun to receive the royalties from them, he sat down to design a locked breech pistol which would satisfy Colt's. He did this so well that about half the military pistols in the world still use his system or a minor variant of it, and his Colt design was only retired by the US Army in 1985.

The perfected Browning system of breech locking is generally referred to as the 'swinging link' system. In his first successful design the barrel was carried in the frame by two hinged links, one attached to the breech and one to the muzzle. Around the barrel was the slide, and in the undersurface of the slide top were two slots. The upper surface of the barrel, above the breech, had two raised lugs which matched these slots. At the rear of the barrel was the breechblock with firing pin, and on the frame was a hammer. To load the pistol a magazine was slid into the butt; then the slide was pulled back to its fullest extent and released. The return spring, underneath the barrel, drove the slide forward, picking up a cartridge and entering it into the chamber. As the breechblock closed up behind the loaded cartridge, so the thrust moved the barrel forward. Because of the hinged links, as the barrel went forward, so it rose, and the lugs entered the slots in the slide. Barrel and slide were thus locked together as the hammer fell and the cartridge was fired. On firing, the barrel and slide both began to move back under recoil, and they stayed locked together long enough to allow the bullet to leave the muzzle and the chamber pressure to drop. By then the rearward motion of the barrel, constrained by the hinged links, caused the barrel to drop, pulling its lugs free from the recesses in the slide. The barrel stopped, the slide continued back to eject the case and cock the hammer, and then it started forward again to repeat the cycle.

Browning's design was taken by Colt's and appeared as their Model 1900, chambered for a new .38 calibre cartridge. About 12,000 were made, the US Army taking 210 and the US Navy 70 for trial. There were some minor faults and Colt's set about cleaning up the design which appeared again as the Model 1902. This had a hold-open catch which held the slide back after the last round had been fired, indicating that the gun was empty, and it also introduced the 'inertia' firing pin. The original Model 1900 had a firing pin which, when the hammer was down, pressed against the cap of the loaded cartridge, a dangerous condition in which to carry the weapon. In the 1902 model the firing pin was shortened; when the hammer was down, and pressing against the rear end of the pin, its front end did not protrude through the firing-pin hole in the breechblock, so that it could be safely carried in that condition. The fact that the firing pin actually hit the cap when the hammer was dropped by pulling the trigger was simply due to its inertia; the hammer gave it such a blow that it flew to the front with sufficient force to fire the cartridge, then it rebounded back into the breechblock until the next hammer blow. The 1902 was a good design and it stayed in production until 1929, but although the military showed interest they did not adopt it.

The military had made up their minds that nothing under .45 calibre would do; they had recently gone through the Spanish-American War and the subsequent Philippine Insurrection largely armed with the .38 revolvers which Colt's had developed for them in the early 1890s, and their experiences were salutary. Crazed Moro tribesmen charging with swords proved unstoppable with .38 bullets, and only a hurried purchase of .45 revolvers had restored the Army's faith in handguns. In 1904, in a spirit of scientific enquiry, Colonel John T. Thompson

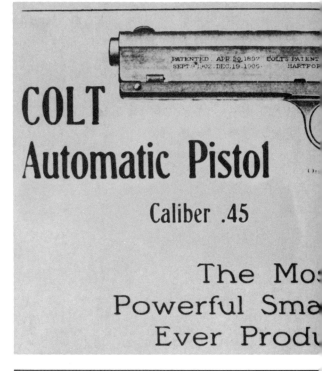

COLT
Automatic Pistol

Caliber .45

The Mos
Powerful Sma
Ever Produ

(who later developed the famous Thompson submachine-gun) and Colonel LaGarde were detailed off to fire a collection of military pistols of various types and calibres into cattle, horses and even corpses, in order to determine some fundamentals about the wounding and stopping-power of bullets. Their report makes gruesome reading, but they proved, at least to the US Army, that nothing less than .45 calibre need be considered for use in combat.

Colt's responded to this by first designing a new .45 rimless cartridge suitable for use in automatic pistols. Once they had this, they enlarged their 1902 pistol to suit and submitted it for test; so confident were they that they actually laid out the production lines ready to start as soon as the Army approved the design. But although the Army bought 200 for test, no orders followed. As the 'Model 1905', the first Colt .45 automatic went on commercial sale instead, and about 6,000 of them were made over the next six years.

Although the US Army turned down the Model 1905 – among other reasons, because it had no safety device – they nevertheless saw enough good in it to suggest that it could well point the way to a replacement for the existing

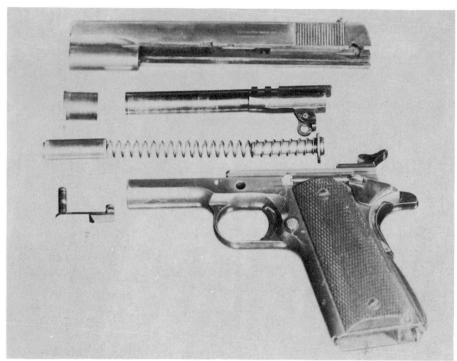

48. A contemporary advertisement for the first of the .45 Colt-Brownings, developed in 1905.

49. The major components of the M1911A1, a modification of the M1911 accepted in 1926. Note the link attached below the breech end of the barrel, which controls the tipping movement, the two locking lugs in the upper surface.

revolvers, and on 28 December 1906 the Chief of Staff ordered a Board of Inquiry set up to carry out tests which would decide on the Army's future pistol. The Chief of Ordnance had already advertised the forthcoming trials to the major manufacturers in both the USA and Europe, specifying that nothing less than .45 calibre would be considered.

On 15 January 1907 the Board assembled at Springfield Arsenal to inspect the weapons which had been submitted: the Colt, Parabellum, Savage, Knoble, Bergmann and White-Merrill automatic pistols, the Colt and Smith & Wesson revolvers, and the Webley-Fosbery automatic revolver. The Colt was a slightly improved Model 1905; the Parabellum was of normal 'New Model' design (which was about to be tried by the German Army and become the Pistole '08) but in .45 calibre; the Savage was an American design using a rotating barrel to obtain a very brief period of breech locking –

indeed, it could almost be considered as a delayed blowback; the Knoble and White-Merril were American designs which never got any further; and the Bergmann was the Bergmann-'Mars' in .45 calibre.

The testing was thorough but expeditious – far more expeditious than a comparable trial would be today – and in May 1907 the Board made its report. The Knoble and Bergmann were rapidly disposed of; the Knoble was 'so crudely manufactured as to render any test without value', while when the Bergmann was tried 'the blow of the hammer was insufficient to discharge the cartridges and the test was discontinued'. The White-Merril 'was so unsatisfactory that the test was discontinued' and the Webley-Fosbery, though it passed all tests with flying colours, was rejected on the grounds of difficulty of loading from horseback and the absence of a double-action trigger mechanism. The conclusion was that the Colt and Savage pistols were of sufficient merit to warrant the purchase of 200 of each to be issued for extended troop trials. The Parabellum was 'not recommended for service test because its certainty of action . . . is not considered satisfactory'.

The Chief of Staff authorized the purchase of the 400 pistols, but Savage were unwilling to set up a production line to make 200 pistols without assurances that more orders would be forthcoming. The DWM company were then approached to supply 200 Parabellum in .45 calibre, but they, too, were unwilling to make such a small number. It is probable that they knew that they were about to receive a massive order from the German Army and did not want to tie up plant on such a small order. Eventually Savage agreed to produce the required 200; Colt's were quite happy to produce their share, and six troops of cavalry were outfitted with the two types of pistol.

Some months of practical use showed that while neither pistol was perfectly satisfactory, the Colt showed more promise than the Savage, and the company were asked to redesign the pistol to incorporate some modifications which the soldiers thought desirable. By this time the Ordnance Department had designed a cartridge with a heavier bullet than the original Colt pattern, and, using this as the basis, Colt's made the changes. Further trials followed, and in 1911 the Colt .45 Pistol M1911 was formally adopted for service.

50. John Browning's most famous design: the US Army's .45 M1911 service pistol. This specimen was made under contract by Remington during the First World War.

51. The rotating-barrel .45 Savage was a close contender for adoption by the US Army in 1907–10, but ultimately lost out to the Colt.

52. The Nambu-designed 8mm 'Taisho 4', or Fourth Year pistol, was approved by the Japanese Army but never officially purchased.

The changes that had been carried out made the pistol safer, simpler and more reliable. The principal change was in the method of mounting the barrel and unlocking it. Instead of using two links, one at the muzzle and one under the chamber, the new design used only one, beneath the chamber, and held the muzzle in alignment by means of a bush inserted into the front of the slide. There was sufficient clearance in this bush to allow the barrel a small amount of angular movement, so that when the pistol was fired the slide and barrel moved back as before, but the link caused the rear end of the barrel to drop and thus disconnect the lugs from the slide, the barrel pivoting about the muzzle bush. A manual safety catch was fitted to the frame, a grip safety to the rear edge of the butt, and the hammer was given a half-cock notch.

The magazine held seven .45 cartridges and an eighth cartridge could be manually loaded into the chamber over a full magazine.

There was only one other country in the world where an automatic pistol was being developed for military use in the early years of the twentieth century, and that was Japan. The Japanese Army had adopted a 9mm revolver known as the Type 26 in 1894; the terminology came from the fact that 1894 was the 26th year of the current emperor's reign. It was a hotchpotch of Smith & Wesson and other features, and it was to stay in production until about 1924, in service until the end of the Second World War. But in 1897 a Captain Kijiro Nambu had been detailed to the Army Arsenal at Koishikawa, Tokyo, and had shown himself to be a gifted designer. He improved the standard Army rifle, and then in 1902 began designing an automatic pistol. Although the resulting Nambu pistol externally resembles the Luger to some degree, and its locking system resembles the Mauser to a similar degree, in fact it is quite an original design.

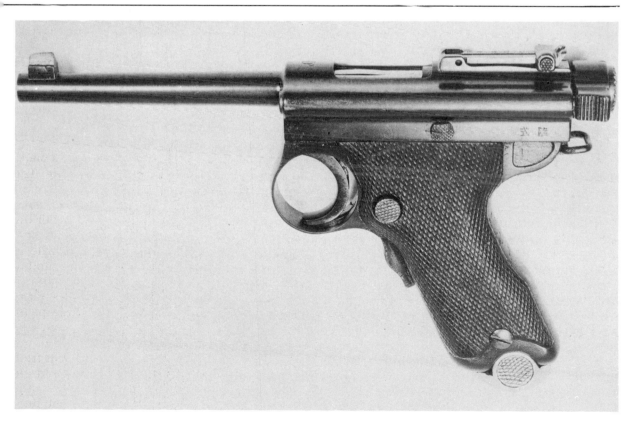

53. The 'Baby Nambu', a scaled-down version of the Fourth Year Pistol in 7mm calibre, was favoured by senior oficers.

The Nambu pistol has a barrel and barrel extension moving on top of a butt and frame unit. Inside the barrel extension is the bolt, cocked by pulling back on a pair of 'wings' at the rear end, the bolt contains the firing pin; there is no hammer. The magazine fits into the well-raked butt and contains eight rounds of a specially developed 8mm bottle-necked cartridge. The barrel extension carries, pivoted beneath it, a hammer-shaped locking block. When the pistol is ready to fire, the lower end of the hammerhead rests on a lug in the pistol frame and the upper end is forced into a recess on the underside of the bolt. On firing, bolt and barrel unit recoil together for a short distance, at the end of which movement the locking block is carried off the frame lug so that the hammerhead can swing downwards, aided by a spring. As it moves down, so the upper end is pulled free from the bolt recess; the barrel and extension stop moving and the bolt is free to recoil and carry out the reloading cycle. As the bolt closes, so the locking block is carried forward by the movement of the barrel extension, lifts on to the frame lug and re-enters the bolt

recess. At the same time, the firing pin is held by the sear, ready to be released by the trigger.

The Nambu had a single return spring mounted alongside the bolt, in a tunnel in the frame. There was no manual safety catch, but a grip safety was let into the front edge of the butt, underneath the trigger guard. Some of the early production models had the rear edge of the butt grooved to fit a wooden holster-stock, similar to that developed for the Mauser pistol, but this was later discontinued.

The latest research has now proved that production of the Nambu began as early as 1906, but it was not formally adopted for military use; officers were permitted to purchase them privately, and many did so, but the first formal adoption came from the Japanese Navy in 1909. Formal Army adoption did not come until 1915, and by that time the pistol had been slightly modified to simplify production and improve reliability.

3
THE MILITARY REVOLVER IN THE TWENTIETH CENTURY

One might be forgiven for supposing that by the end of the nineteenth century the revolver had gone about as far as it could go. It was reliable, robust, came in all sizes and one or two odd shapes, and was a universally-accepted weapon. But the designers still had some ideas up their sleeves, and although the fundamental shape and principle has not altered in the past eighty-odd years, there has been a steady improvement in design and, in particular, in methods of manufacture. Though it must be said that the improvements are generally aimed at simplifying manufacture, making manufacture less expensive and labour-intensive, and making the weapons safer. Except for a handful of examples, the standard of workmanship and finish of revolvers in the 1980s can rarely be considered as perfect as that found in the revolvers of the 1900s.

We left the revolver when the American manufacturers had developed the solid-frame design with side-opening cylinder to a point where it had been accepted by military users. By 1900, there were two methods of securing the cylinder and its associated crane in general use: one, due to Colt, locked the cylinder by means of a pin passing through the cylinder arbor and into the standing breech, releasing it by pulling back a thumb-catch on the side of the frame below the hammer; the other, due to Smith & Wesson, used a similar central pin, but anchored it both in the standing breech and to a lug beneath the barrel, releasing it by a thumb-catch which had to be pushed forward. The advantage claimed for the Smith & Wesson version was that it secured both ends of the cylinder axis against movement and was therefore theoretically more solid.

Good as this may have been, Smith & Wesson were not entirely satisfied with it, particularly for heavy-calibre revolvers, and in 1908 they introduced their .44 Hand Ejector First Model; this is more commonly known as the 'Triple Lock' model, because of the addition of a third locking point to secure the cylinder and crane

into the frame. This took the form of a special catch fitted into the front end of the frame, just ahead of the cylinder, and the front lock was reinforced by a shroud beneath the barrel into which the entire length of the ejector rod fitted, with the usual locking catch at the front end. As might be imagined, getting all three of these locks to operate in perfect synchrony was a masterpiece of fitting, and the clearances are like those on a good watch. Some critics feel that S&W were over-egging the pudding by adding the third lock, but whatever the opinion, there is no doubt that the weapons were exceptionally strong and superlatively finished. Very few revolvers since then have had anything like as perfect an appearance as the Triple Lock models. First produced in .44 calibre, they later appeared in .45 Colt, .450 Eley, .44-40 Winchester and .44 Russian chambering.

The Philippine Insurrection having shown the US Army that their .38 revolvers were insufficiently powerful, they had hurriedly bought

54. The 'Triple Lock' of the Smith & Wesson New Century revolver.

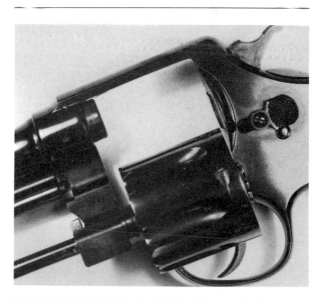

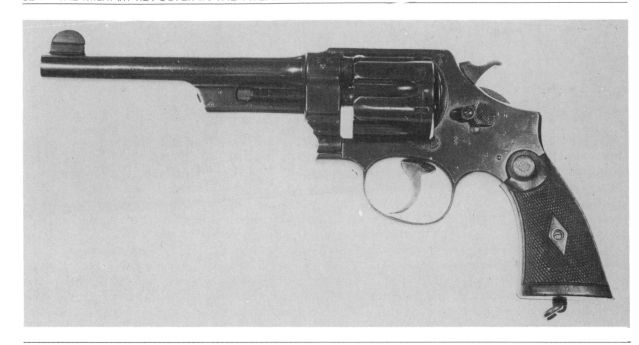

55. The .455 S&W Century, as purchased by the British Army in 1915.

56. The Webley Mk VI revolver, last of the .455-calibre patterns.

57. The 'Pistol, Old Pattern' manufactured for the British Army by Garate, Anitua y Cia in Spain (1915–17).

up whatever .45 revolvers they could lay hands on. Colt's responded to this emergency by developing, in 1898, their 'New Service' revolver. This was a large-frame model designed, with an eye firmly upon military adoption, to be capable of firing the heaviest loads. Originally designed for the .45 Colt cartridge, it was eventually made in eighteen different calibres from .38 to .476 Enfield, and with several different barrel lengths. The US Army bought several thousand, and it was to remain in production until 1940 by which time more than 336,000 had been made.

When the First World War broke out in 1914 the demand for pistols among the combatants was enormous. Britain turned to the USA and in 1915 purchased 5,000 Smith & Wesson Triple Lock models specially chambered for the .455 Webley cartridge. These were excellent weapons until they met the mud and dirt of the trenches; it was then found that the tolerances of the carefully crafted Triple Lock were such that the slightest amount of dirt on the locking surfaces would prevent the revolver from being closed and hence fired. They were rapidly withdrawn from front-line service and replaced by Webley revolvers.

Meanwhile Britain had been searching elsewhere for revolvers, and about the only place she could go was to Spain. Here the output of

revolvers was large, but the quality was poor, and eventually only two Spanish models were selected. Both were in .455 calibre and specially made for the British Army contract. The first was by Garate Anitua y Compania of Eibar; it was a top-break double-action revolver bearing a strong resemblance to the Smith & Wessons which had been commercially marketed in the 1890s in smaller calibres. The other was made by Trocaola Aranzabal y Compania, also of Eibar, and was practically identical with the Garate model. These two pistols were formally approved for British Army service as the 'Pistol Old Pattern No 1 Mark I' and 'No 2 Mark I' in November 1915, but it is doubtful whether many were purchased because very few have survived.

The year 1915 also saw the arrival of what was to be the last of the Army Webleys, the Mark VI model. This was much the same as the previous five Marks, though it had a 6-inch barrel, the grip was slightly flared at the bottom and the foresight was a loose leaf pinned into the barrel. As soon as it had been approved, in

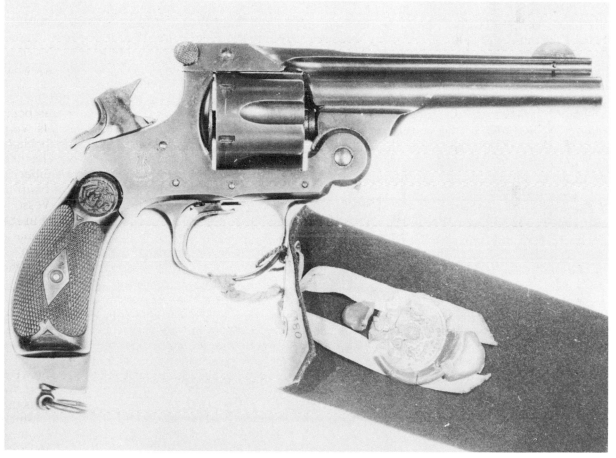

May 1915, Webley's were given orders to produce as many as they could, and during the next three and a half years they turned out an average of 2,500 revolvers a week. By the time this production was under way the mobile war had settled down to trench warfare and the demand for revolvers also settled down as fewer were lost, so that having taken up the slack with the Smith & Wesson and Spanish orders, the army's requirements were satisfied by Webley's production for the remainder of the war.

In 1917 the Americans found themselves at war and found themselves totally unprepared for it. One of the first demands was for thousands of pistols, and although numerous companies were given contracts to manufacture the Colt M1911 automatic, it was soon discovered that signing a contract does not immediately produce armaments. Factories have to be set up, workers trained, and the bugs have to be eradicated from the production line before anything worthwhile can happen, and this process takes time. It seemed logical, therefore, to turn to the two great revolver makers and ask them to produce revolvers, for which they were fully tooled-up, to fill the gap until the automatic pistols began to flow. There was, however, one slight snag. Because the army had standardized on the .45 automatic pistol, it had also, obviously, standardized on the .45 Auto Colt Pistol (ACP) cartridge. So any revolver purchased had to be in .45 calibre and fire the automatic pistol cartridge.

The drawback to this was simply that the .45 ACP had no rim to prevent it falling all the way through the cylinder, and no rim to catch on to the extractor star so that the empty cases could be ejected. The Ordnance Department got around this by devising the 'half-moon clip', a spring clip which held three .45 ACP cartridges by their extraction grooves and at the correct spacing so that they would drop into three chambers of the revolver cylinder. Two clips-full and the revolver was loaded; when the extractor rod was pushed back it bore against the clips and the six empty cases were ejected. It was then necessary, if possible, to pick up the ejected assemblies and reclaim the clips so that another six rounds could be loaded.

The half-moon clip wasn't a bad idea, but it meant that the revolver cylinder had to be

shortened, since with the clips fitted the .45 ACP cartridge protruded farther behind the cylinder than did a conventionally rimmed cartridge. So with one modification and another, the army finally got its revolvers from Colt's and Smith & Wesson, both called the 'Model 1917' and both widely issued. More than 150,000 from each maker were accepted by the Army before the war ended.

It is worth noting that many thousands of these M1917 revolvers were sold off as surplus in the post-war years, and since the civilian customers found the half-moon clip and the .45 ACP cartridge requirement somewhat restrictive, cartridge manufacturers were quick to develop a .45 revolver cartridge with an extra thick rim. This could be loaded into the cylinder in the same way as a conventional revolver cartridge and the thick rim took up the space behind the cylinder and ensured that the cap was in the right place to be struck by the firing pin. These were called '.45 Auto-Rim' and were manufactured for many years afterwards.

When the First World War ended the military revolver was in the minority. America, Germany, Austria and Italy had all adopted automatics before the war and had shown that they were capable of standing up to the rigours of service life, and even if the French were still officially armed with the Model 1892 revolver, they had purchased more than a million automatic pistols during the war and intended to make it their future standard. Only Britain remained wedded to the revolver, and even she was having second thoughts.

The war had shown the British Army that there was a fundamental drawback to a heavy-calibre revolver, and that was the amount of time and ammunition it required to teach a soldier how to use it effectively. And under wartime conditions, time and ammunition were the two things which trainees didn't have much of. From civilian suit to front-line trench was a process of no more than six months, often less, and the number of things which had to be crammed into the recruit's head in that time left

58. The .455 New Service Colt revolver, with a 5.5in barrel, 1915.

59. The .45 M1917 Colt revolver, made for the US rimless automatic pistol cartridge and issued with half-moon clips. Note the larger than normal gap between the back of the cylinder and the frame.

60. The Swiss Ordonnanzrevolver 82/29 W+F, a simplification of the earlier 1882 pattern, was adopted for NCOs and men ineligible for the Parabellum-type 06/29 W+F automatic pistol.

very little for practise with the revolver. So that when the young officer (for common soldiers rarely got their hands on a revolver in the British Army) was confronted with his first live target, he usually missed it and suffered the consequences.

Despite the traumatic time the Americans had had in The Philippines in the 1890s, the British Army reached the same conclusions as had the Americans in the 1880s; the calibre was too big, the pistol too heavy, the recoil too great. By reducing the calibre and increasing the velocity the terminal energy would still be more than enough to deal a lethal blow, and the revolver would weigh less and give less recoil, and would therefore be easier to learn to use.

This decision was reached in 1922, and the British Government commissioned Webley to carry out experiments. Webley's patterned their design on a civilian .38, but incorporated various features from the .455 Mark VI; they submitted their revolver to the Army, confident that it would mark the start of a fresh sequence of Webley designs, but got a rude shock when the Army turned it down. They got an even ruder shock shortly afterwards when the Royal Small Arms Factory at Enfield produced its own design of .38 service revolver. Apart from some

very minor details it was virtually the same as Webley's; but since none of the features of the Webley were patent protected – they having expired years before – there was very little that Webley could do about it. The new revolver was taken into service in 1927 though it did not receive formal approval – as the 'Pistol, Revolver, No 2 Mark I' – until 1932. It was accompanied by a new cartridge of .38 calibre which carried a solid lead 200-grain bullet with a blunt nose, an attempt to wring as much stopping power as possible out of the calibre. But there were doubts about the legality of this bullet, and whether it was within the bounds of The Hague Convention of 1899. This had laid down that 'explosive bullets' should be outlawed; in this context 'explosive' does not mean filled with a detonating substance, but that the bullet will deform violently when striking flesh and so cause an unnecessarily savage and painful wound. There were stories from the First World War about Germans dealing somewhat harshly with captured British officers in possession of soft lead .455 bullets, though there is no evidence to support these old soldiers' tales. In 1938 the lead bullet was withdrawn and a jacketed bullet issued in its place.

One more change came to the Enfield revolver before the outbreak of the Second World War. During the inter-war years revolvers were issued widely to troops of the Royal Tank

61, 62. The British Army adopted the Enfield-made 'Pistol No. 2 Mk I' in .38 calibre. The later No. 1 Mk I* had the hammer spur ground off to prevent snagging in tanks, vehicles or confined spaces.

Regiment, since rifles are unhandy things to carry inside tanks and submachine-guns were virtually unheard-of. The troopers found that the hammer of the Enfield had a habit of catching in various fittings inside the tank, particularly when they were attempting to climb out through a small hatch, and damage was being regularly done to the revolvers. So in June 1938 the 'Mark I' was issued. This was the same revolver, but with the hammer spur ground off to leave a smooth surface which had nothing to snag on projections. It also meant that there was no way to thumb the hammer back, and therefore the Mark I* was a self-cocking only revolver. The mainspring was lightened to give an easier trigger pull, and the grips were formed with thumb-recesses to give a better grip, but even so it was a difficult pistol with which to shoot accurately. For reasons of standardization, existing Mark I pistols were converted to Mark I* when they went through workshops for repair or servicing, and for that reason it is uncommon to find an original Enfield Mark I pistol today.

It was ironic that when the war broke out, Enfield could not supply revolvers fast enough to equip the Army and Webley's were called in to manufacture their original 1923 design for military use.

At the outbreak of war in 1939, Britain's was the only major army to retain a revolver in first-line military service; several countries held them in reserve stocks and were to bring them out for use by rear-echelon troops during the course of the war, but only Britain relied entirely on the revolver. And, of course, the combined production capacity of Enfield, Webley and lesser contractors such as Albion Motors could not keep pace with demand, so that in 1940 the British Purchasing Commission in the USA was once more knocking on Smith & Wesson's door. The result was the Smith & Wesson .38/200 revolver, specially developed for the British Army. It was, in fact, the standard S&W 'Military and Police' Model, which had been in manufacture since 1899 with minor variations, but with the chambers designed to accept the standard British .38 cartridge. A total of 568,204 of these revolvers were supplied to the British and Commonwealth armies prior to 29 March 1945. Apart from a tendency to misfire, they were very well liked by British soldiers, since they were far more handy and had a smoother trigger action than the issue Enfield revolvers. The liability to misfires was entirely due to the caps of British military ammunition being harder than those of

American commercial ammunition; since the Smith & Wesson hammer mechanism had been designed for American caps it occasionally refused to fire a British one, but this could usually be cured by altering the tension of the hammer mainspring by a thoughtfully provided tensioning screw in the front of the handgrip.

A very similar revolver was also made by Smith & Wesson for the US Army: this was the 'Victory Model' which was primarily for issue to guards, security police and similar personnel in the United States so as to relieve the demand for .45 automatic pistols. More than 800,000 of these were manufactured.

When the war ended in 1945, the British were to retain their revolvers in service for a few more years and only one other army took a revolver into use as their first-line arm – the army of the newly formed state of Israel. In the late 1940s, fighting for their existence against Arab states, they needed pistols and were unable to buy a standard model in the requisite quantities. They therefore settled on the simplest reliable design they could find and manufactured a copy of the Smith & Wesson Victory Model. But since .38 ammunition was scarce in Israel, and 9mm Parabellum ammuni-

tion was easy to obtain, they copied the idea of the American M1917 revolvers and chambered the gun with a short cylinder which would take 9mm cartridges held in half-moon clips. This effective revolver served the Israelis well for a few years until they were able to obtain a modern automatic pistol. And at about the same time that the Israelis took it out of service, so the British Army also retired their Enfield revolver in favour of the Browning automatic pistol, and the revolver, as a first-line military weapon, had reached the end of its run.

This is not to say that revolvers are not to be found still in military use; aircrews, for example, often carry revolvers since they are light and, to be honest, few airmen ever contemplate the situation in which they are liable to be called upon to use handguns. But the heavy-calibre, robust, often ugly, pure military revolver has been completely ousted from the inventories by the automatic pistol. And so it is to the automatic pistol that we must now return.

63. As usual, wartime demands exceeded manufacturing capacity in Britain, and thousands of these .38/200 Smith & Wesson models were purchased in the USA. They were to remain in use until the mid 1950s.

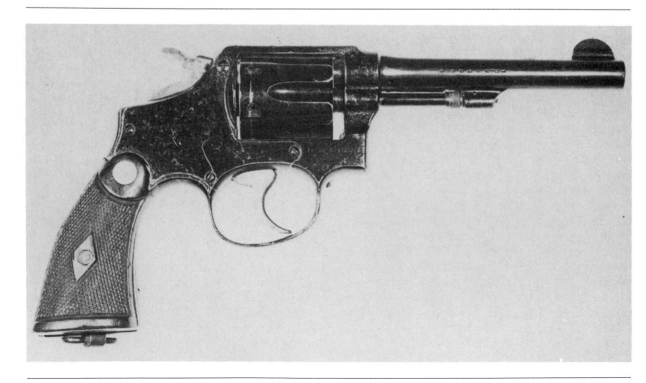

4

MILITARY AUTOMATIC PISTOLS, 1914–45

The First World War saw very little innovation in automatic pistols; a major war is no time to start fooling around with something as relatively unimportant as pistol design when things like machine-guns and automatic rifles are far more vital. The only pistol problem during a major war is that of providing sufficient of them for the vastly expanded armies. This was made worse in the 1914–18 war by the need to arm far more people with pistols than had hitherto been considered necessary. In pre-war days the usual distribution was to officers, senior non-commissioned officers and cavalry troopers. In wartime it was found necessary to issue them on a wider scale, to machine-gunners, mortarmen, aviators, tank crews, armoured car crews and similar occupations which came into being

64. The 'Ruby' automatic pistol, purchased in the hundreds of thousands in Spain by France and Italy.

as a result of the expansion of military technology.

The first to feel the pinch were the French, and in early 1915 they sent an emissary to Spain to seek an automatic pistol. In the gunmaking town of Eibar he found a company called Gabilondo y Urresti who contracted to supply the French with 10,000 pistols a month, a figure which was soon increased to 30,000.

Gabilondo & Urresti were like most other Eibar gunmakers, virtually an assembly plant for components made at home by an infinity of sub-contracting individual workmen. They had begun operating in 1904, making cheap revolvers, and in 1910 began to make a copy of the Browning 'Baby' 1906 blowback pocket pistol in 6.35mm calibre which they called the 'Radium'. In 1914 they increased the size of the weapon, turning it into a copy of the Browning 1903 model in 7.65mm calibre; this they called

the 'Ruby' and this was the pistol they were to supply to the French. It was a simple, roughly-made blowback automatic, firing a bullet that could hardly be considered a manstopper.

Moreover, Gabilondo had not the slightest possibility of making the required quantity of pistols themselves, but rather than forego a relatively easy profit they took the contract and promptly sub-contracted it to five other local companies. Even this proved insufficient when the contract figure went up to 30,000 a month, and more local firms were brought in. It was the chance of a lifetime for many of them and was to prove the foundation of their post-war operations, since the basic design was kept in production until the mid 1930s and sold cheaply throughout the world. The French got their automatic pistols, even if the Spanish firms had to scurry around to get things organized, and soon the Italian Army became interested in a similar contract.

The Italian Army, although still outfitted with Bodeo revolvers, had also adopted an automatic pistol just before the outbreak of war. This was the 9mm Glisenti, a weapon of mysterious origin, usually credited to the Italian designer, Revelli, but, perhaps, owing something to the earlier Swiss Häussler-Roch pistol. It was chambered for a special 9mm cartridge which, though the same shape and size as the 9mm

65. The Glisenti pistol, Mo.910, was used officially by the Italian Army prior to the First World War. It fires an under-powered version of the 9mm Parabellum owing to its somewhat weak construction.

66. The Brixia pistol was a cleaned-up commercial variant of the Glisenti, known to the army as the Mo.912.

Parabellum, was loaded to a lower velocity. This was necessary since the Glisenti is not a particularly strong design. Like the Nambu and Mauser, the Glisenti uses a barrel and square barrel extension moving on top of a butt and frame, with the bolt moving inside the barrel extension. There is a locking wedge pivoted inside the butt frame and when the bolt is closed this is vertical and passes through a slot in the barrel extension to engage in a recess in the bolt. On firing, this wedge holds barrel extension and bolt together as they recoil for a distance of about 7mm; at this point the gradual turning of the wedge, due to its lower end being fixed to a pivot, takes the top end out of the bolt recess, thus permitting the bolt to open as the barrel and extension stop. A return spring sends back the bolt, loading a fresh round from the magazine in the butt, and the forward movement of the barrel extension rotates the wedge and re-locks it into the bolt.

This sounds perfectly satisfactory, and is, except for the fact that the frame of the pistol is

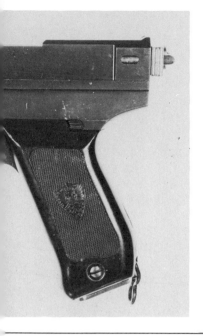

three-sided; the left side is merely a cover plate which gives no structural strength to the pistol, and therefore the firing stresses are unevenly distributed and an excessive pressure can damage the pistol. This excessive pressure is easily obtained by firing a standard 9mm Parabellum cartridge or two; and since the two cartridges are interchangeable and almost indistinguishable, this is precisely what happened in many cases. And, because only a small number of Glisenti pistols had been manufactured before war broke out, and because of their general unreliability, the Italian Army had to begin looking elsewhere for pistols, which is why they turned to Spain.

The Italians, though, had some local gunmakers who were available for military production. One of these was Pietro Beretta of Gardone Val Trompia near Brescia, and in June 1915 Beretta took out a patent for 'Innovations for Automatic Pistols'. From this came the Beretta Model 1915 pistol and the foundation of a long line of excellent weapons. Although Beretta's had been in the business of making firearms since 1577, this was the first time they had manufactured a pistol.

The Beretta 1915 was a simple but well-made blowback design in 7.65mm calibre. A notable feature was the cutting away of the front end of the slide over the barrel, leaving only a small

67. Italy's demands for automatic pistols gave Beretta the chance to offer this, the blowback 1915 model, and begin a dynasty.

strip of metal to support the foresight. Behind this cutaway portion was a conventional ejection slot in the slide top. Ejection of the cartridge was, unusually, performed by the firing pin; as the slide ran back it cocked the internal hammer, and the pressure of the hammer against the rear of the firing pin during this movement forced the pin forward so that it acted on the base of the cartridge to eject it. The Model 15 was immediately adopted by the Italian Army and shortly afterwards a variant model chambered for the 9mm Glisenti cartridge was also manufactured. Although still using the blowback principle, this model was given a stiffer return spring so as to withstand the more powerful cartridge.

After some experience had been obtained with the Model 1915, Beretta made some changes: the small ejection port was removed, since it tended to catch ejected cases and jam the pistol. Instead, the entire slide top was cut away from the rear of the ejection port to the front sight mounting, setting a pattern which has remained the standard for Beretta military pistols ever since. This was the Model 15/19 and it, too, became Army standard.

68. The 1934-model Beretta equipped the Italian forces throughout the Second World War.

Beretta gradually made improvements to the basic design. In 1923 they placed an external hammer on the pistol, because, generally speaking, military users prefer external hammers since they give an instant indication of whether or not the weapon is cocked. In wartime such refinements are often overlooked, as on the 1915 and 1915/19 models, but with the return of peace the external hammer was demanded. Finally, in 1934, Beretta produced what was to be the standard Italian service weapon for many years. The 1934 model was much the same as the previous one, but was enlarged slightly to take the 9mm Short cartridge. This small round, less powerful than the 9mm Parabellum, allows the pistol firing it to be

a blowback, but it still fired a respectably sized bullet at a practical velocity, and by 1934 was becoming very popular throughout Europe, as will be seen. There was also a 'Model 1935' Beretta's produced for the Italian Air Force which was simply the 1934 in 7.65mm calibre.

The First World War led to the map of Central Europe being re-arranged and to the foundation of new states; and one of the first priorities of these new states was to attend to their defence, form and equip armies and procure weapons. All began this by sharing in the millions of weapons sequestered from the

Germans and also by taking a share of weapons from the countries that had been their former masters. This inevitably meant that the armed forces finished with a hotch-potch of weapons of every shape, size, age and calibre, and by the middle 1920s they were anxious to try and bring some order to this chaos.

The first people to make this move were the Czechs who probably had the worst mixture of weaponry, and in 1924 the Ceskoslovenska Zbrojovka (Czech Arms Factory) which had been set up in 1919, began making a new Mauser rifle for the Czech Army. To do this it obtained assistance from the Mauser factory and Engineer Josef Nickl went to Czechoslovakia. Nickl, as it happened, was a frustrated pistol designer; he had designed a pocket pistol for Mauser, but due to the war it had not been developed. He now interested the Czechs in the design and in 1922 it went into production as the CZ22 or 'Nickl Pistol' for the Czech Army. It was a neat design in 9mm Short calibre, using a

rotating barrel to lock the breech into the slide, though in that calibre a rotating barrel – or any other form of lock – was quite superfluous. The reason it was there was simply that Nickl originally designed the pistol in 9mm Parabellum, and submitted it for trial in that calibre. The Czech Army, after testing it, asked for further pistols for trial and also for ten specimens chambered for the 9mm Short. It was easier to leave the design as it stood and merely alter the chambering than to redesign the pistol as a blowback.

However, although the firm got an order for 19,000 pistols, their production left something to be desired since there was far too much handfitting in the manufacture. The Czech Army wanted a weapon with totally interchangeable parts, and after a great deal of argument production was shifted to the Ceska

69. The Czech CZ22 pistol was designed by Josef Nickl, who had worked for Mauser prior to the First World War.

70. The CZ24 was an improved model of the Nickl pistol, but retained the same rotating barrel-lock even though the weak cartridge didn't need it.

71. The CZ24 field-stripped. Note the locking lugs on the barrel and the cam-block which lay in the frame.

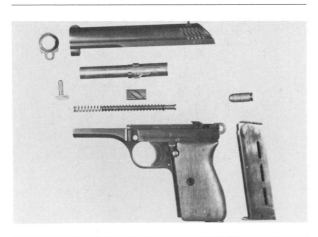

Zbrojovka (Bohemian Arms Company) in Strakonice which was subsequently to be responsible for all Czech pistol manufacture. The chief designer at the new plant made some slight changes in the Nickl design to suit his manufacturing system and the result was re-christened the CZ24 and about 20,000 pistols were made. After this contract was completed he took a hard look at the design. Seeing no good reason for perpetuating the rotating barrel in a weapon of low power, he completely redesigned it as a blowback pistol, though keeping the same outward appearance. This became the CZ27 pistol, produced concurrently with the CZ24 but issued to the Czech police and treasury guards rather than the armed forces. Several hundred CZ24 pistols were also sold to Lithuania and about 1,700 of a slightly modified 'WZ/1928' variant went to Poland.

In 1936, the Czech Air Force expressed dissatisfaction with the CZ24, and this was echoed by the Army; they claimed it was too expensive and too complicated and demanded something cheaper and easier to operate. Myška, the designer at Strakonice, therefore developed a completely new design which was adopted as the CZ38. This was much larger than the CZ24 though it fired the same cartridge; was a straightforward blowback pistol; had a self-cocking lock, which meant it could only be fired by pulling through on the trigger to cock and fire the hammer in one movement; and was unusual in having the barrel hinged to the front of the frame so that it could be more easily cleaned. The weapon cost only 270 crowns (£2.26 at the 1936 rate of exchange) instead of 545 crowns (£4.57) for the CZ24, but although production started in 1938 not one pistol ever reached the Czech forces before the German occupation of the country in early 1939. Although more than 40,000 were eventually produced, they were almost all taken by the German Army as reserve pistols.

72. The CZ38 field-stripped, showing how the barrel is hinged to the frame. There is a hammer, but the design of the slide was such that it was impossible to reach it. Thus, the CZ38 fires only in the self-cocking mode.

73. The CZ38, designed by Frantisek Myška, was intended to replace the CZ24. However, only small quantities were made for the Czech Army before the German invasion, and more than 40,000 surviving guns were issued to the Wehrmacht.

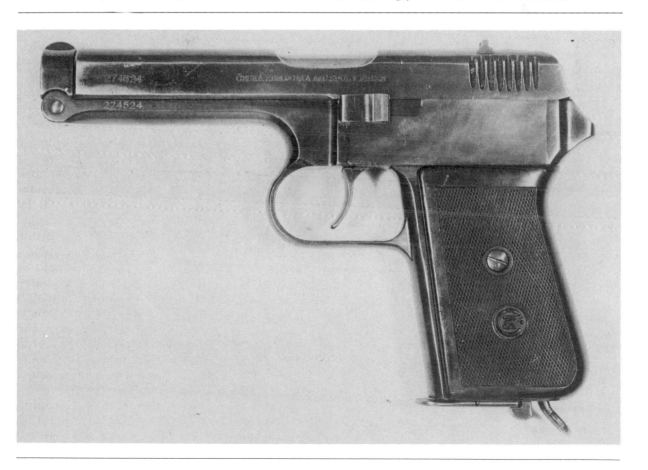

74. The Frommer 'Stop' pistol of 1912 was another complicated design which went to great lengths to lock the breech against a weak cartridge.

Hungary had also become independent of Austria, and took with it the pistol it had used during the war, the Frommer M1912 or 'Stop'. This had been issued to the Honved, the Hungarian element of the Austro-Hungarian Army (the Austrian element used the Steyr 1911), and was another peculiar design. It had been developed by Rudolf Frommer, a contemporary and friend of Georg Roth and Karel Krnka, and although proof is absent, it is likely that Frommer was influenced by Krnka. His 1912 pistol uses the long recoil system of operation, with a rotating breech bolt, but, as with the Nickl design, the complication seems hardly worth the effort since the cartridge used was the 7.65mm Browning. There was an external hammer and a grip safety, but no applied safety catch, and feed was from a removable box magazine in the butt, in the conventional way. It is an extremely complicated little pistol, but for all that it proved reliable and capable of standing up to the rough and tumble of military service, and the Hungarian Army continued to use it throughout the Second World War even though simpler designs were replacing it.

It was probably the cost of such a complex pistol which led the Hungarian Army to demand a new one in the late 1920s and Frommer obliged by producing his 'M1929'. This was a very simple exposed-hammer blowback, retaining the grip safety and firing the 9mm Short cartridge, an improvement on the 7.65mm round so far as military use was concerned. Then in 1937 came Frommer's last design, adopted as the 'M1937', which was little more than the M1929 cleaned up and made slightly easier to manufacture. During the war the Luftwaffe had 85,000 of these M1937 pistols made for them in 7.65mm calibre, though they also demanded the addition of a manual safety catch on the left side of the frame.

Further to the east, the Soviet Government spent the 1920s in building up the strength of the Red Army after the debilitating effects of the Great War and the subsequent civil war. They kept the pre-war M1895 Nagant revolver in production, since the machinery was there, but they required something more modern and as early as 1923 they had begun testing various designs from Russian factories and elsewhere. These continued throughout the decade, but all came to naught when in 1929 the Artillery Committee ruled that any future pistol was to fire the 7.63mm Mauser cartridge, and not the 7.65mm Browning which the tested pistols had all used. The Mauser had become familiar in Russia after the purchase of numbers of Mauser Military pistols in the early 1920s, and it appealed to the Artillery Commission because it

75. Frommer saw the light and, in 1929, produced this simple – if inelegant – blowback for the Hungarian armed forces.

76. The last pistol developed from Frommer's designs was the Model 1937. Adopted by the Hungarian Army, and supplied in appreciable numbers to the Germans during the war, the 1937-pattern is mechanically the same as its '1929' predecessor – but rather more handsome.

would provide a powerful pistol and also a cartridge suitable for use in submachine-guns.

In 1930, Fedor Tokarev, a weapon designer of long standing, appeared with a new design of pistol which, after considerable testing, was adopted in 1931 as the TT-30. In fact, it was simply a near-copy of the Browning Colt, using the same sort of swinging link to disengage lugs on the barrel from recesses in the slide. The only noteworthy features were that the hammer and its mainspring could be slipped from the frame for cleaning, and the frame carried carefully machined lips which guided the cartridges from the magazine, so that the magazine lips were not so critical to the loading reliability as on other designs. It is believed that about 95,000 of the TT-30 were made by 1935 when the design was slightly changed to speed up production. In the original model, as in the Browning designs, the locking ribs were machined on the top of the barrel. Tokarev changed this to machining two concentric ribs all round the barrel. This made no difference to the operation, but it meant that the locking ribs could be machined as the barrel exterior contour was being formed on a lathe, rather than as a separate operation on a milling machine. Taking one machine and process out of the production schedule can make a considerable difference to speed and cost, and the modification was forthwith approved. The new design became known as the TT-33, and went into mass production in 1936. How many hundreds of thousands were subsequently manufactured is not known.

Moving now to Scandinavia, Finland purchased 9,000 'Ruby' automatics from France in 1919 and had adopted the 7.65mm Parabellum

77. The Soviet Tokarev, developed in 1930 and still in wide use.

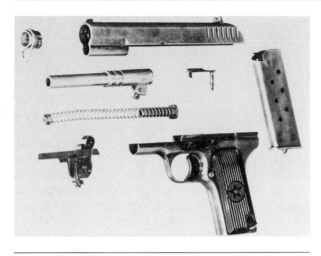

pistol in 1923, but in the late 1920s decided to develop a weapon of its own. The pistol finally adopted was designed by Aimo Lahti, who had been working as a designer for many years and had developed machine- and submachine-guns. He had his pistol ready for production in 1932, but it was not until 1935 that it was taken into use as the 'Lahti M/35'. The Lahti looks a little like a Parabellum, having a similarly well-shaped butt and exposed barrel, but mechanically it is closer to a Bergmann or Mauser. The barrel is attached to a square-section extension on top of the butt and frame, and the bolt, inside the extension, is locked by a U-shaped steel block which engages in both bolt and extension. On firing, the entire barrel unit recoils for a

78. The second- or 1933-pattern Tokarev field-stripped. Note that the locking lugs on the barrel are entirely circumferential, and how the lockwork is cleverly 'packaged' in a removable sub-assembly.

79. This is a 'Tokagypt', a 9mm Parabellum Hungarian-made variant of the Tokarev for the Egyptian Army. Although this makes more sense than the original 7.62mm pistol, it failed to catch on.

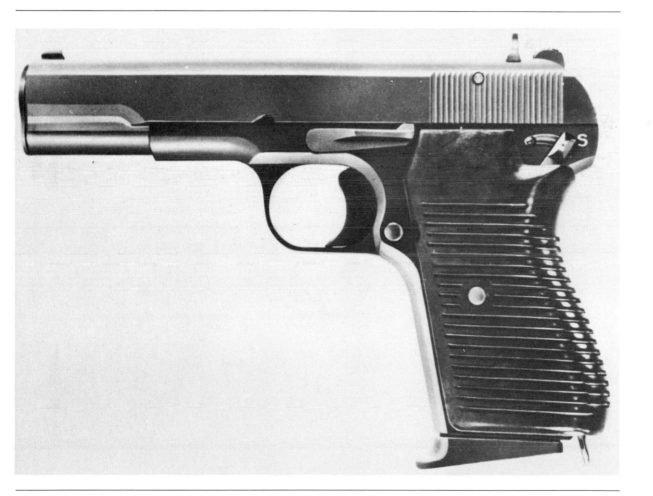

short distance, until the block is forced up by a ramp on the frame, so allowing the bolt to move backwards while the barrel comes to a stop. What is particularly interesting about the Lahti is that there is an accelerator, a fitting more usually found on machine-guns. It consists of a simple pivoted arm just behind the breech; when the barrel unit recoils, and just as the bolt is unlocked, the lower end of this arm strikes an abutment on the frame so that it pivots, and its upper end presses against the front of the bolt. Due to the position of the pivot, the upper end of the lever moves through a greater arc than does the bottom, so that it gives the bolt a sharp blow, speeding up the opening and adding a very positive impulse to the latent energy given by the recoil. This means that, for example, in extremely cold weather such as is common in Finland, there is no danger of thick oil slowing up the bolt or causing a malfunction. The accelerator overcomes any problems from thick lubricant, weak cartridges, dirt or fouling, and the Lahti is among the most reliable pistols ever made. Chambered for the 9mm Parabellum cartridge, the Lahti has been the standard Finnish service pistol ever since; it was also adopted by the Swedish Army after supplies of the Walther HP had been severed in 1940.

In Belgium, Fabrique Nationale was busy producing its range of Browning blowback pistols, but its design office was occupied in perfecting John Browning's last pistol design. Browning had begun thinking about improvements almost as soon as the Colt M1911 had been accepted for service in the USA, but the outbreak of war had interrupted him and he had subsequently devoted most of his time to machine-gun and automatic rifle work. With the war over, he returned to his pistol and set about making it simpler. In June 1923 he applied for a US patent, which showed that he had made a change in the locking system; instead of using the swinging link, he achieved the same result by a simple lug of steel beneath the breech into which a sloping slot was cut. This slot surrounded a locking pin which passed through the frame, so that as the barrel and slide recoiled, the pin, acting on the slope

80. The Lahti pistol, adopted by the Finnish Army in 1935, was later accepted by the Swedes as the 'M/40'. One of the Swedish Husqvarna-made guns is shown here.

of the slot, would pull the rear end of the barrel down, so pulling the usual locking lugs on the top of the barrel away from the recesses in the slide. In other words, the method of locking was the same as in the Colt M1911 design, but the mechanism of unlocking was different and simpler.

Another change (generally regarded as for the worse) was that the trigger was no longer connected to the hammer by a yoke passing around the magazine, as in the Colt pistol. One of Browning's aims was to simplify, and he now placed the lever connecting trigger and striker sear in the slide, so that unless the slide was fully forward and the breech locked, the lever was not properly aligned and thus the trigger would not operate the striker. It will be seen that by using a single component he had disposed of two, since there was no longer any need of a separate disconnector.

Browning took his design to Belgium, for the FN design office to clean up the minor details and complete the development to production stage. Here Dieudonné Saive, the chief designer, made some changes. First, he developed a double-row magazine for thirteen 9mm Parabellum cartridges, giving the pistol a remarkable capacity in reserve. Then he did away with the striker mechanism contained in the rear of the slide and substituted an external hammer. Browning agreed with these changes, but before anything more could be done, late in 1926 Browning died. Saive continued with the development and by 1928 had perfected the design and tested prototypes. Manufacture would commence in 1929.

Unfortunately the bottom fell out of the stock market in 1929 and the depression gripped Europe; FN felt the pinch like every other manufacturing plant and was forced to lay off workers. The launch of the new pistol had to be postponed, and it was not until 1934 that the company felt confident enough to set up production lines and announce the pistol. It was

82. A GP35 variant with a tangent-leaf back sight.

immediately taken into service by the Belgian Army as the 'Model 1935, Grand Puissance' from which it has since been variously called the 'GP-35' or 'Hi-Power'.

The GP35 was an immediate success, sales being made to Belgium, Lithuania, China and Peru before war broke out in 1939. Two models were produced, the 'Ordinaire' with a fixed-notch backsight, and the 'Adjustable Sight Model' which had a tangent leaf sight graduated to 500 metres and had a slot in the rear of the butt to take a shoulder stock. There was also a variant of this model with the sights graduated to 1,000 metres, a fine piece of optimism no doubt calculated to impress the less technically knowledgeable members of banana republic purchasing commissions.

At almost the same time as the Browning GP35 appeared, a similar weapon had been independently developed in Poland. Like the

Czechs, the Polish Army had a collection of weapons of various types and decided to settle on a standard issue. In 1929 the Department of Armaments decided to buy a licence to manufacture the CZ24 pistol, but there were various objections, from the Army and from Polish experts, that the design was over-complicated and fired too weak a cartridge. Spurred by the announcement, two Polish designers, Wilniewczyc and Skrzypinski, set about developing a design which would employ the Browning method of breech locking and use the 9mm Parabellum cartridge. Mindful of Browning principles, and the prototype GP, they came up with the idea of using a shaped lug beneath the breech acting against a cross-pin in the frame to lower the rear of the barrel during recoil, and so unlock the breech. A grip safety was fitted behind the butt, but there was no applied safety catch. The first prototype was made in 1931, and after some testing the Polish Army requested that a release lever be fitted which

would permit the hammer to be safely lowered on to a loaded chamber; with the hammer cocked, pressing this lever first locks the firing pin and then drops the hammer. When needed for firing a quick thumb-cocking of the hammer releases the firing pin and the pistol is immediately ready. The hammer does not have the usual thumb-spur but ends in a serrated ring; according to legend this was so that the cavalry could cock the hammer by simply pushing the pistol down against their breeches. There is what appears to be a safety catch at the rear of the frame; this is merely a locking catch which holds the slide back to allow dismantling.

The pistol was approved for service as the 'Vis', a corruption of the designers' initials, but it is more often called the 'Radom' from the name of the Polish state factory which manufactured it. About 18,000 were made before the outbreak of war, and these can all be easily identified by the Polish eagle engraved on the slide. During the war manufacture continued

83. A Polish Army Radom, or wz.35, pistol

84. The Radom field-stripped, showing the unlocking cam under the breech; this gun was manufactured under German supervision and carries an additional German 'P.35 (p)' slide mark plus several Waffenamt inspectors' marks

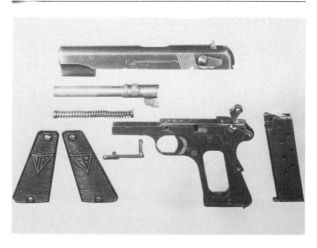

under German control; these pistols were to a poorer standard of finish and did not have the eagle, merely being marked 'Pist. 35(p)' with a German acceptance stamp.

It is a strange coincidence that 1935 saw the introduction of three pistols which all relied upon some degree of modification to Browning's Colt M1911 design. The third of these was the French Army's Modèle 1935.

The French had had some unfortunate experiences with weaponry during the First World War and in the 1920s they began a house-clearing, getting rid of the worst wartime weapons and seeking new designs. As we have seen, they had purchased cheap Spanish blow-back automatics by the thousand during the war, and the Army decided that a good automatic pistol was needed to replace these. The state factory at Saint-Etienne made some experimental pistols in the 1920s, but they had their hands full developing machine-guns and rifles and were not inclined to press the pistol very hard, so nothing came of it. Eventually, in 1934, the Government called for a competitive

trial to select a suitable pistol. One difficulty was that the pistol had to chamber a new cartridge which Saint-Etienne had designed, a peculiar 7.65mm 'Long' which resembled no other 7.65mm in existence and, in truth, was not a particularly good cartridge. Among the few entrants (for many companies were not sufficiently interested to submit designs in a weird calibre that would be unsaleable elsewhere, and foreign companies were also alive to the fact that the chances of the French adopting a non-French design were zero) was a Browning GP35 chambered for the 7.65mm round and a design from Saint-Etienne, but the one which was selected for development came from the Société Alsacienne des Constructions Mécaniques (SACM) and had been designed by a man called Charles Petter.

Little is known of Petter; he was Swiss by birth, served a term in the French Foreign Legion, was invalided out after being wounded

85. The French Army's Mle 1935, made by SACM, chambered the weak 7.65mm Longue cartridge.

in North Africa and eventually became an engineer at SACM. He took out a patent for his pistol – similar in some respects to the GP – in 1934, and the basic design is that of the M1911, using the same swinging link method of un-locking the breech. The only significant dif-ference is the designing of the hammer unit so that it can be removed from the frame for clean-ing and repair. The pistol was well made and finished, with a particularly well-shaped butt, though the safety catch was rather primitive, simply a half-round shaft on the slide which, when revolved by a simple lever, blocked the hammer's fall.

The SACM factory finally went into produc-tion in 1938, the French Army having ordered 10,500 pistols, but by the time the Germans captured the area in 1940 only 3,500 had been manufactured. Under German control manufac-ture was continued, about 40,000 being pro-duced for the German Army.

In 1938, fearful that production by SACM would be insufficient, the Manufacture d'Armes de Saint-Etienne (MAS) redesigned the Modèle

35 so as to make it easier to mass produce. The basic mechanical features remained the same, but the outline became more angular and the finish was to a lesser standard. The barrel locking system was changed from Browning's ribs and recesses to a single heavy lug above the chamber which locked into the ejection recess in the slide, a very simple system and probably the first time this was done in a pro-duction pistol. This design was called the Modèle 35S and production was put in hand at four factories: Saint-Etienne (MAS), Tulle (MAT), Châtellerault (MAC) and Société d'Applications Générales Electriques et Mécaniques (SAGEM). However, only a small number had been made before the German occupation, and thereafter manufacture ceased, to be revived again after the war for a short time.

In 1937 SACM sold limited rights to the Petter patent to the Swiss company, Schweizerische

86. The Mle 1935.S was a simplification of the Mle 35 A, made by the French government at Saint-Etienne. The German invasion prevented large-scale deliveries.

Industric Gesellschaft (SIG), and in the following year sold them a licence to produce Petter designs for commercial sale outside France. SIG eventually improved the design and it became the basis of their successful post-war range of pistols.

During this period, the Swiss Army adopted what was to prove the last major variation of the Luger pistol – the much simplified Ordonnanzpistole 06/29 W+F, developed by the Eidgenössische Waffenfabrik at Berne to replace the earlier 1906-type guns. However, the Swiss accepted that the Luger was complicated and expensive to make; consequently, while the pistols were adopted for officers and senior NCOs in November 1929, a cheap revolver (known as the 82/29) had already been accepted for lower-ranking NCOs and men. The principal recognition characteristics of the perfected Swiss Luger are its plain-surface toggle-grips, safety-catch button and dismantling-catch head, the straight-front butt and the plainer receiver. The first production guns were delivered in 1933, work continuing until 1946 by which time it was clear that the SIG-Petter was a more than adequate replacement

for the antiquated Borchardt-Luger design. A few pistols were produced for commercial sale, ending in 1947.

Japan had a unique incentive to design a new automatic pistol: in 1923 the Tokyo arsenal which produced the original Nambu pistol was destroyed by an earthquake. Responsibility for pistol production was shifted to Nagoya Arsenal and a commission was set up to develop a fresh design, aided by Colonel Nambu. In effect they took the original Nambu and simplified it, making it easier to produce, though their eventual design was still somewhat over-complicated for what it did. Instead of a single return spring on one side of the bolt, the new design was provided with two, one on each side of the bolt. The grip safety was abolished and a manual safety catch fitted, though it was positioned at the front of the frame where it needed the firer's other hand to operate it. There was also a magazine safety device, which prevented

87. First issued in 1933, but known as the Ordonnanzpistole 06/29 W+F, the Swiss Parabellum was the last major derivation of Luger's design to be officially adopted. This gun is a 9mm conversion, dating from the trials against the SIG-Petters in the early 1940s.

firing the round in the chamber if the magazine was removed; a fixed rear sight replaced the original adjustable sight; and the grip was made slightly thinner. So modified, the pistol now became the '14th Year Type' and was introduced in 1925, the 14th Year of the Taisho Era. It received a further modification in the mid 1930s as a result of experience in Manchuria; the trigger guard was enlarged so that it could be used by a man wearing heavy gloves.

Although the Type 14 pistol was officially adopted, it met with a mixed reception; officially issued to NCOs, it was merely 'recommended' to officers who were required to provide pistols at their own expense, and since the Type 14 was heavy and bulky they preferred to purchase imported European small-calibre automatics which, into the bargain, were cheaper. Colonel Nambu became aware of this problem and in 1929 began designing a smaller weapon which would still fire the standard Japanese 8mm cartridge. He put together a prototype in 1931 then passed the weapon to the Army Ordnance Office for

88. The Nambu-inspired 14th Year Type pistol was widely issued in the Japanese Army. This gun has the post-1939 large or 'Manchurian' trigger guard. Note the inconveniently placed safety lever on the slide of the slide above the trigger.

further development. They decided to make it even smaller and lighter and, in the process, ruined Nambu's good design and made the pistol even more expensive to produce than the Type 14. But, bureaucracy being what it is, once the system had begun to function it was impossible to stop, and the modified pistol went into production in 1934 as the 'Type 94'. (The system of nomenclature for Japanese weapons had changed; instead of being numbered after the year of the current Emperor's reign, they were now numbered according to the year of the Japanese calendar, and 1934 was the Japanese year 2594.)

The Type 94 differed from any previous Nambu design and from any other pistol in existence. It was a locked breech pistol which had a slide enclosing the barrel and forming the breechblock, the barrel being locked to it by a

89. The Japanese Type 94 pistol, an awkward and badly-designed weapon.

steel wedge. This held slide and barrel together for a short recoil stroke, then dropped into a recess in the frame, so stopping the barrel but freeing the slide. As the slide returned to load a fresh round, it pushed the barrel forward and lifted the wedge up to re-lock the two components together. The original production models were well finished, of good material, and the breech locking system was sound, so that on the face of it the pistol is a good one. But the shape and appearance are odd, to say the least, and it does not, somehow, feel good in the hand. More serious, though, is the fact that an aberrant design makes them quite unsafe. First, the sear, connecting the trigger with the hammer, lies in the side of the slide and can be depressed by gripping the slide too firmly, so firing the pistol should it be loaded and cocked. Secondly, the design of the locking system was such that it was possible to fire the weapon even if the breech had failed to lock – as, for example, because of dirt preventing movement of the locking wedge. These problems became more pronounced during the war when quality

of materials and workmanship declined. Even so, the Type 94 was popular with its users, largely because it was lighter and easier to carry; though the young officers still complained about the price.

It will be recalled that the Spanish Army had adopted the 9mm Bergmann-'Mars' in 1905, buying about a thousand Schilling-made weapons before supplies halted. These guns were subsequently replaced by the Pieper-made Bergmann-Bayard, deliveries of which did not commence until 1909. By 1912, however, a local designer had begun to impress the military procurement department with a new weapon.

Lieutenant-Colonel the Count de Campo-Giro had begun work on a pistol as early as 1900, and by 1904 had a working prototype. It had a curious tubular barrel which makes it resemble an air pistol, but it fired a special 9mm cartridge of Campo-Giro's own design and had a locked breech which depended upon a laterally sliding wedge, moved by a cam track in the pistol frame. After some testing and analysis, modifications were made, notably changing the calibre to suit the 9mm Bergmann-Bayard cartridge which was now the official Spanish pistol round – under the name '9mm Largo' – and some alterations to the frame outline to make the pistol more comfortable to hold. The perfected design was returned to the Spanish Army in 1910, tested successfully, and a small quantity of Campo-Giro pistols was made at Oviedo in 1912. The army experts suggested more changes, the most important of which was the complete removal of the breech lock, turning the pistol into a blowback – but still firing the 9mm Largo, one of the most powerful pistol cartridges ever made. This was done by using an exceptionally strong return spring and also adding a recoil absorber in the frame which reduced the impact of the slide on recoil. This final version was given formal approval in 1913 and was adopted as the 'Modelo 1913' in January 1914.

The perfected Campo-Giro pistol was manufactured under contract to the Spanish Army by a company called Esperanza y Unceta of Guernica. During the 1914–18 war they also produced numbers of cheap automatics for supply to France and Italy and adopted the trademark 'Astra'. During the war years, according to fragmentary reports, some technical problem appeared with the Campo-Giro pistol which led to some serious firing accidents; the Count of Campo-Giro had died as the result of a riding accident in 1915, so Esperanza y Unceta set about redesigning the pistol to try and remove the cause of the accidents. The redesign retained the distinctive tubular appearance, but put the hammer inside the frame, strengthened many parts, and made the pistol easier to dismantle and clean. The resulting design went into Spanish service as the 'Modelo 1921' and was sold on the commercial market as the 'Astra 400' for many years. A smaller version, the 'Astra 300' was made in 7.65mm or 9mm Short chambering, and during the Second World War some 82,400 of these were supplied to the Luftwaffe. A second

90. It may resemble an air pistol, but this is the Mo.1913 Campo-Giro blowback automatic adopted by the Spanish Army.

variant was the 'Astra 600' chambered for the 9mm Parabellum cartridge, and about 10,500 of these were made for Germany from 1943 to 1944.

The Astra company also manufactured copies of the Mauser Military pistol for many years – and they were not the only Spanish firm to do so. During the 1920s the terms of the Treaty of Versailles made life difficult for German gun-makers and therefore their pre-war markets were open to all comers. Several Spanish firms realized that copies of the Mauser would do well in China, where the Mauser had always been popular with warlords who liked impressive weapons. Moreover an embargo on rifle shipments to China meant that heavy pistols with shoulder-stocks were in demand. The Astra 900 looked exactly like the Mauser C/96, but the internal arrangements were very different, designed for ease and cheapness of manufacture rather than for engineering elegance. Instead of the self-contained removable firing lock, the Astra had a removable plate on the left side and all the lock mechanism pinned to the right side of the frame. The breech lock-

ing system was also slightly different. There was also a 'Model 901' which had a selective fire switch on the left side of the frame. This allowed the weapon to be fired in the full automatic mode at about 850 rounds a minute, which emptied the magazine in about seven-tenths of a second and usually spread the bullets all over the scenery.

And so at last we come to Germany, where pistol design and production was to undergo some remarkable ups and downs during the years under review. At the outbreak of war in 1914, the 9mm Pistole '08 was the standard, as we have seen, and it was in full production in two factories, that of DWM at Berlin-Char-lottenburg and that of the government-run Erfurt Rifle Factory. The DWM factory was turning out some 700 pistols per day at its peak in 1915.

A second Parabellum pistol had been adopted for service in 1913; this was the 'Long

91. The replacement for the Campo-Giro was the Mo.1921, commercially touted as the Astra Mo.400, which remained the Spanish Army's service pistol until long after the end of the Second World War.

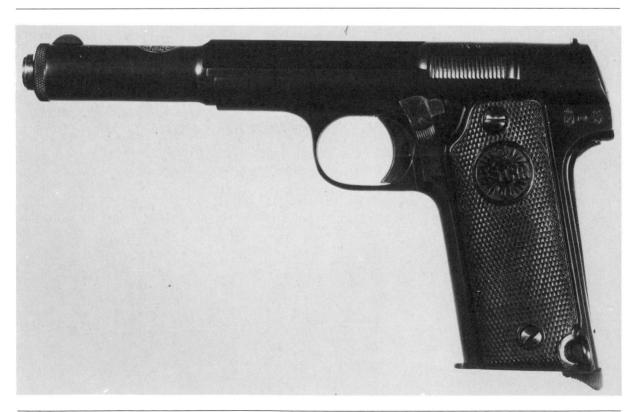

'08', more commonly called the 'Artillery Model'. It was similar to the '08 model, but had a long (20cm) barrel and a tangent backsight graduated to 800 metres. Each pistol had a wooden stock, upon which was strapped the leather holster, and the stock could clip to the rear of the butt for use as a carbine. These pistols were originally for issue to NCOs and men of the ammunition columns, though their issue appears to have become more widespread during the war. In 1917 a drum magazine holding 32 rounds was introduced; this had a long 'tongue' which entered the butt of the pistol and turned it into a semi-automatic carbine of considerable capacity. These were often issued to storm-troops for trench raiding and in 1918 were issued to crews of torpedo-boats and minesweepers.

The production of Parabellum pistols could not satisfy the demand for handguns, and since the Parabellum was difficult to manufacture, and only two sets of manufacturing machinery existed in Germany, recourse had to be made to other sources of supply. Mauser was ordered to produce 150,000 of its C/96 pistol chambered

for the 9mm Parabellum cartridge, Bavaria bought 20,000 9mm Steyr-Hahns, and other manufacturers were given substantial orders for simple 7.65mm blowback pistols. Among these were the Beholla, Menta and Leonhardt (all the same design but made to military order by different factories), the Langenhan and the Dreyse pistols. By absorbing these and by raking up all the Reichsrevolvers which had been stored away, the German Army managed to keep itself supplied with pistols until the war ended.

And with the end of the war came the Treaty of Versailles and the Allied Disarmament Commission, both of which severely restricted the activities of all manufacturers of warlike material in Germany for several years. The armed forces were restricted in size, which meant that the stock of Parabellum pistols on hand would more than suffice to meet their needs for some time to come. DWM was forbidden to trade with the German Army, and

92. Production of the German P.08, the Parabellum, continued well into the Second World War. This is a Krieghoff-made gun, supplied to the Luftwaffe in 1936.

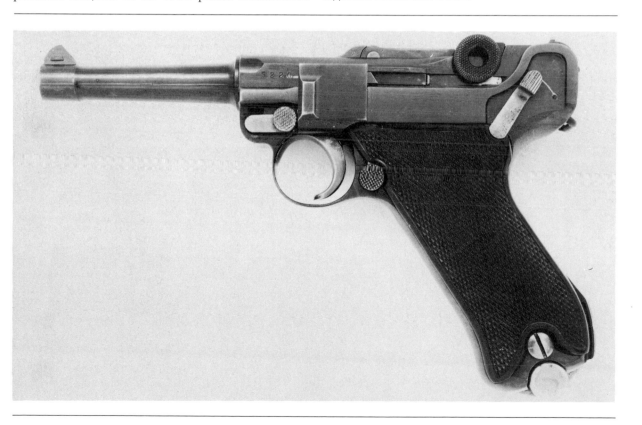

therefore a new company, Simson & Cie of Suhl, received the official contract to refurbish weapons and supply the army with new pistols from time to time. Simson then acquired the old Erfurt manufacturing machinery, though some 'new' pistols were actually made from stocks of war-time parts manufactured by DWM.

Restrictions gradually relaxed and DWM, which by now had changed its name to become the Berliner-Karlsruhe Industriewerk (BKIW), began exporting Parabellum pistols in 1923, beginning with Finland and later supplying The Netherlands. But part way through the Dutch contract BKIW were taken over by a consortium which included the Mauserwerke, and in a rationalization programme the entire production line for the Parabellum pistol was transferred to the Mauser factory at Oberndorf on 1 May 1930, ending DWM's connection with the Parabellum pistol.

In 1933 the Nazi Party came to power and rearmament began. Mauser and Simson were given contracts for the refurbishment of pistols.

Several years earlier, the Army Ordnance Office had introduced a coding system under which the manufacturers of any military equipment would be indicated by code marks on the products. Mauser was now allotted the mark 'S/42' but, in 1935, Simson sold what machinery it had to Krieghoff and the latter, having re-tooled, began production for the Luftwaffe. (The Simson machinery had come from Erfurt when that factory was dismantled under the orders of the Allied Disarmament Commission in 1919.)

But the Army was having doubts about the Parabellum pistol; it was a precision job and an expensive one, and surely, by the mid 1930s it ought to be possible to produce a military pistol which was less expensive, easier to mass produce and, above all, less fussy about its ammunition than the Parabellum. The Army declared its interest and waited to see what came up.

By the early 1930s the most go-ahead pistol manufacturer in Germany was the Carl Walther Waffenfabrik. He had begun making blowback

93. Probably the last of the Lugers: a modern Mauser-made gun, commemorating the 75th anniversary of the Swiss adoption. A wide variety of special guns has been made in the last fifteen years.

94. The Walther PPK broke new ground in both appearance and mechanical operation.

pistols in 1908, and had supplied several to the Army from 1915 to 1918 period. In 1929 he broke new ground with the patenting of the 'Polizei Pistole' or 'Model PP'. This was a fixed-barrel blowback in 7.65mm calibre with an external hammer and a double-action lock, and it was shaped in a streamlined fashion which made every other pocket pistol obsolete overnight. Other innovative features included a signal pin which protruded from the slide to show that there was a cartridge in the chamber, and a safety catch on the slide which, when operated with the pistol cocked, dropped the hammer on to a locked firing pin. Carried in this way, with the hammer down over a loaded chamber, the pistol could be brought into action

by simply pushing off the safety catch and pulling the trigger, whereupon the hammer was cocked and released to fire the first shot; thereafter the recoiling slide cocked the hammer in the usual way. Or, for precision, the hammer could be thumbed back to full cock for the first shot if desired.

The Walther PP was an immediate success and was acquired by several police departments in Germany and elsewhere in Europe; it was followed in 1930 by a slightly smaller model, the 'PPK' for 'PP Kriminal', implying its use by the Kriminal Polizei or plain-clothes detectives. The smaller size of the weapon allowed it to be carried concealed, while the PP was intended for wear in a holster by uniformed police. Both the PP and PPK were eventually purchased in considerable numbers by the Luftwaffe and by the paramilitary forces.

Walther then turned to the question of a 9mm Parabellum pistol for military adoption. He began by developing the 'Model MP' which was simply a 'PP' scaled up to take the heavier cartridge. It seems a logical step to have taken, but I doubt if Walther really thought he had any hope of selling the German Army a blowback pistol in that calibre.

During the mid 1930s, Walther and his principal designer, Fritz Barthelmes, developed the Armee-Pistole ('AP'). Patented in 1936–7, this was a completely new approach and bore no relationship to any previous Walther designs. It was recoil-operated, with the barrel and slide riding above the frame and butt. Beneath the rear end of the barrel, set in the frame, was a locking wedge which was kept up in engagement with the barrel by a spring plunger and a ramp in the frame. The upper surface of the wedge engaged in a recess beneath the barrel, while wings on the outer edges of the wedge engaged in slots in the front end of the slide, which did not wholly enclose the barrel. On firing, barrel and slide moved back together, carrying the wedge back with them until it struck a transom in the frame. The spring plunger then drove the wedge downward, freeing the slide to recoil and complete the reloading cycle. The pistol had an internal hammer with the double-action lock and slide-mounted safety catch of the 'PP'. There were twin recoil springs, let into the side of the frame and acting against the lower edge of the slide.

A handful of Armee-Pistolen was made, but after testing them the Army Weapons Office declared a preference for a pistol with an external hammer, a common military choice for safety reasons. The changes necessitated by this were relatively minor, and Walther was soon back with the exposed hammer 'MP' or Militär-Pistole (the last of several Walthers to bear the name) and then the perfected 'HP' or Heeres-Pistole. The HP was put into small-scale commercial production while undergoing final German acceptance trials, many of these pistols being supplied to Sweden.

A few comparatively insignificant changes were made to the Heeres-Pistole, and the Pistole 38 was finally approved in April 1940 even though production in Walther's Zella-Mehlis factory had actually begun in 1939.

The first Walther-made pistols displayed the company's usual commercial trademark, WALTHER within a scroll (the so-called 'Walther Banner'), on the left side of the slide. Shortly afterwards, a code-marking system was adopted and the pistols were thereafter identified by the number '480' stamped on the slide. This system changed in the autumn of 1940, when Walther was allocated the code letters 'ac'. The authorities soon realized that

95. The Walther P.38, adopted to replace the Parabellum, became the German military standard in 1940 – though it never entirely displaced its predecessor.

96. A 1943-vintage Walther-made P.38, field stripped; the locking block lies between the barrel and the frame. Note also the slender recoil spring set into the frame side. There is another on the opposite side.

Walther's production would not be sufficient to meet demands, and contracts were given to Mauser (then making the Luger), Spreewerke and – possibly – Böhmische Waffenfabrik in 1941. Guns were delivered from Spreewerke of Berlin and Böhmische Waffenfabrik which was the Ce'ska Zbrojovka factory under German control in the first half of 1942, but the latter's interests in the P-38 was quickly reduced to that of a parts-maker. The first Mauser-made P-38 did not appear until the end of the year, which neatly disposes of a popular but mistaken theory that Mauser supervised Spreewerke's tooling after completing its own! The Mauser products bear the code 'byf' or 'svw', the latter in 1945–6 only, post-war production being continued under French supervision; Spreewerke's are coded 'cyq' or 'cvq', the latter being a die with a broken 'y'-tail. Most Walther and Mauser guns also bear the last two digits of the year of production on the left side of the slide.

In addition to the principal manufacturers, several sub-contractors made P-38 parts such as frames, barrels, magazines and hammers. Among the most important was Fabrique Nationale, which is sometimes misleadingly identified as an assembler of complete guns.

The total number of P-38 manufactured during the war has never been accurately determined, owing to the destruction of records – accidental and deliberate – which took place in 1945. The best estimate is that Walther made about 550,000, Mauser about 320,000 and Spreewerke about 250,000, giving a total of 1,120,000.

Despite starting up production of the P-38, Mauser continued to assemble the Parabellum until the end of December 1942. It had accumulated a sufficiently large stock of parts to be able to continue assembling pistols off and on until the end of the war, and even then there were sufficient parts in the factory to permit the French to have about 5,000 Parabellums assembled late in 1945. The last foreign contract to be filled was the provision of about 5,000 7.65mm pistols for the Portuguese Army and about 5,600 9mm guns for Bulgaria in 1943.

While the P '08 and P-38 formed the bulk of front-line pistols, the German Army also adopted a number of pistols which it found in production in the various countries it occupied. Thus the FN factory, under German supervision, made more than 300,000 GP-35 pistols and 360,000 Model 1922 7.65mm pistols; some 400,000 CZ27 were acquired from Czechoslovakia; about 375,000 Radom pistols from Poland; almost 100,000 Hungarian Model 37s; and about 300,000 other miscellaneous pistols of various types were purchased from commercial manufacturers in France and Spain.

97. The Mauser HSc, known to the German forces as the 'Pistole Mauser Neuer Art' or P.M.n.A., was a streamlined double-action blowback which – had it not been for the war – might have given Walther a hard time in the marketplace.

German makers also produced second-line pistols in considerable numbers. Mauser, for example, had developed a modern double-action pocket pistol in 7.65mm calibre, the 'Model HSc', just before the war, and almost a quarter of a million of these blowbacks were manufactured, principally for the Navy and Luftwaffe. A less well-known German maker (at that time) was J. P. Sauer & Sohn; they too had developed a very modern pistol in 1938 and placed it on the commercial market, but within a very short time the war broke out and all production went to the armed forces. The Sauer Model 38H was a most innovative weapon and, but for the war, might well have been a considerable commercial success. The company had made a number of 6.35mm and 7.65mm blowback pistols since 1913 – including the 'Behörden-Modell' of 1930 – and they were widely used by German police forces, but in 1938 it abandoned its previous designs and produced a pistol which, in its streamlined shape, bore some resemblance to Walther's Model PP, though the 38H was rather larger. It also had a double-action lock, but it had a unique de-cocking lever let into the left side of the butt, where it could be conveniently operated by the firer's thumb. With the pistol loaded and cocked, depressing this lever took the pressure off the hammer mainspring so that the trigger could be pressed to release the internal hammer; releasing the de-cocking lever under control then lowered the hammer safely on to the loaded chamber. Once in this condition the firer had two choices: he could simply pull through on the trigger to cock and release the hammer, or by depressing the de-cocking lever once more he could raise the hammer to the full cock position for a deliberate shot.

The Sauer 38H was well-made and finished, and of first-class materials. Although the Sauer company reappeared after the war and recommenced manufacture of firearms, for some unknown reason it chose not to revive the Model 38H, which was a great pity.

98. The Sauer Model 38H which appeared shortly before the Second World War began, might also have been a great commercial success. Note the de-cocking lever emerging from the grip, just behind the trigger.

5

SERVICE PISTOLS
AFTER 1945

By the time the Second World War ended in 1945, the output of pistols by the various combatant nations had gone into millions. As the armies were reduced after the war, pistols were returned to store and it was first thought that there would be very little need to manufacture any more pistols for quite some time. However, when the various combatants recovered from the first post-war elation and began to examine their pistols more closely, several decided that what they had fielded during the war was no longer quite good enough. In general, it was those who had the worst pistols – from the combat-effective viewpoint – that were the first to make improvements.

Taking the post-war development of automatic pistols in chronological order would result in a most involved narrative, doubling back and forth between countries as new models appeared, and leading to thorough confusion. Instead, this chapter will tabulate in alphabetical order the countries that have produced new military pistols since 1945. In this way the gradual development of certain 'families' of pistols will be more apparent; where there is cross-fertilization between designs of one country and another, this will be made clear.

AUSTRIA

Having been part of the Third Reich since 1938 Austria had used its own Steyr M1911 pistols converted to 9mm Parabellum and had also adopted the standard German P-38 in considerable numbers. After the war the P-38 remained their issue pistol; this survived, with periodic refurbishment, into the early 1980s. The Austrians supplemented these with the post-war Walther P-1, but the terms of their Treaty of Neutrality forbade the purchase of weapons from Germany and the guns were acquired from Manurhin. As it happened, though, the Steyr-Daimler-Puch factory returned to the weapons business and in the 1970s produced a new pistol in 9mm Parabellum calibre, the Pistole 18. This used an unusual method of delayed blowback operation: the fixed barrel had an enlarged section about midway along its length, and this fitted tightly into a cylinder formed in the slide. Small ports ran from the bore through the barrel wall so that when the pistol was fired a proportion of the propelling gas was diverted into the slide cylinder. This high-pressure gas pressed against the 'piston' formed by the barrel and thus resisted the opening of the slide until the bullet had left the barrel and the accumulated gas was able to be driven back through the ports into the barrel and exhausted to the outside atmosphere.

For various reasons Steyr licensed this pistol for manufacture in the USA, but the American makers were not successful with it and the P 18 was withdrawn from the market. Steyr made some small changes in the design and re-launched it as the 'GB' pistol. It has an external hammer, a polygonally rifled barrel and a magazine which holds no less than 18 rounds. One might expect this to be something of a handful, but in fact it is comfortable to hold and the gas delay system absorbs a lot of the recoil, making it very pleasant to shoot.

In the early 1980s the Austrian Army decided that a new pistol was necessary and, because of the restrictive terms of their country's neutrality, was circumscribed in its choice. The requirement was therefore advertised in Austria, and the general opinion was that the Steyr, as the sole contender, would be selected. To the surprise of most people a completely unknown company (insofar as firearms went) won the contract to supply 25,000 pistols and thus the Glock 17 has been adopted as the Austrian Army pistol.

The Glock is representative of the most modern technology. It uses a skeleton steel frame which is given the required shape by moulded plastic; the slide is also plastic-coated and several of the minor parts are plastic. (It might be said that this has led to some panic that such a pistol could be smuggled past airport X-ray machines; tests have shown that

this can only happen if the machine operator has seriously defective eyesight.) The breech locking is done by the usual Browning cam beneath the barrel, and the barrel locks into the slide not by the usual lugs and recesses but by having the rear of the barrel machined into a square lump which lifts up and locks into the ejection port in the slide, an idea which appears to have been taken from various SIG designs. The pistol fires the usual 9mm Parabellum cartridge and the magazine holds 17 rounds. Like many modern designs of pistol it has no manual safety catch; safety is performed automatically by a locking bar which securely locks the firing pin unless the trigger is pulled back sufficiently far to release the hammer. As the trigger reaches the let-off point it lifts the firing pin lock long enough to allow the hammer to drive it forward. As the trigger is released after the shot, so the lock re-engages and the pistol is safe until the next time the trigger is pulled.

BELGIUM

Fabrique Nationale really had a head start over everyone else in 1945, since it had one of the most modern pistol designs. After most of the production machinery had been retrieved from Germany and Poland, it was able to get the GP-35 back on the market again with minimal delay. With minor modifications to suit individual customers, it was eventually adopted by

99. The Steyr GB is a rare example of gas-delayed blowback operation.

100. The new Austrian Army pistol is the Glock 17, about 40 per cent of which is plastic.

more than 55 different countries as their military standard pistol, a record never matched by any other handgun.

Throughout the 1950s and 1960s, FN kept the GP-35 in production, but turned its design and development attention to rifles and machine-guns, to very good effect. In the 1970s, though, with new designs of automatic pistol appearing in other countries, it was obvious that they would have to do something to keep their position. Since the most significant feature of the new generation of pistols appeared to be the double-action lock, the Browning Hi-Power was now re-designed to incorporate such a lock. However, there were other desirable features – or so various authorities claimed – and therefore the 'Browning Double Action Family' was conceived (after the failure of the abortive 'Fast Action' project), a ringing of the changes which would provide alternatives capable of satisfying virtually any requirement. The 'family' was announced in the early 1980s.

There are three pistols in the family: the basic weapon is the BDA-9S 'Standard', which is the familiar Hi-Power GP-35 fitted with a double-action lock, a larger trigger guard shaped to allow a two-handed grip, and a de-cocking

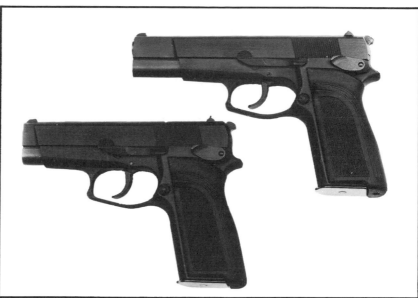

lever/safety catch which is duplicated on both sides of the weapon – one of the frequently asserted requirements of many forces being an 'ambidextrous' safety catch suitable for use by right- or left-handed firers. Next comes the BDA-9M 'Medium' model which uses the frame and butt of the BDA-9S, but with a shorter barrel and slide, so producing a somewhat more compact weapon. Finally there is the BDA-9C 'Compact' which has the barrel and slide of the Medium model on a specially built frame with a shortened butt to produce an extremely small pistol still capable of firing the 9mm Parabellum cartridge. All models take the usual 14-shot magazine, while the Compact model also has a special 7-shot magazine suited to its smaller grip.

For those who prefer the original single-action mechanism, FN now manufacture the 'High-Power Mark 2', which is the same as the pre-war pistol but for the provision of an ambidextrous safety catch, anatomical grip, and wider sights.

CHINA

In pre-war days the Chinese Republic used a variety of pistols which have never been properly categorized, though the Mauser C/96 was very popular, and copies of this, and of the Browning M1900 and M1903 were locally manufactured to varying standards of quality.

101, 102. Two members of the FN-Browning Double Action 'family' – the BDA-9S (standard, 101) and the BDA-9M (medium, 102).

103. The third member of the FN-Browning family is the 'compact' model, the BDA-9C, here seen with a full-length magazine in place.

After the Communist regime had taken over the country and the Nationalist Army had fled to Taiwan, the two forces polarized according to their super-power support; the Communists turned over to complete acceptance and standardization of Soviet weapons, while the

Nationalist force was supplied entirely from US sources. As a result the Communists used the Tokarev TT-33 pistol, calling it the 'Type 54', while the Taiwan troops adopted the .45 Colt M1911A1, though they still had large numbers of the Browning Hi-Powers which had been made for them in Canada during the war.

After the honeymoon with Moscow had palled, the Chinese once more turned to their own resources and began developing their own weapons, though many of the designs used Soviet models for inspiration; thus their 'Type 59' pistol is a copy of the Soviet Makarov and is chambered for the 9×19mm cartridge, known as the 'Type 59' cartridge in China. One design, however, was entirely original; the 'Type 64' pistol.

The Type 64 astonished the Western world when it was first found in Vietnam, for it was obviously a pistol designed for the purpose of assassination and nothing else. It carries an integral silencer built into the frame and covering a fixed perforated barrel. The slide, behind the barrel and really an over-large breechblock, can be locked to the breech or left free to move back under the blowback effect of the special 7.65mm cartridge. This cartridge resembles the universal 7.65mm Auto Colt cartridge, but on closer examination will be seen to be entirely rimless rather than semi-rimmed, and its loading is also non-standard in order to ensure correct working of this odd pistol. If the breech is left unlocked and the pistol is fired, the slide goes back, ejects the spent case and reloads ready for the next shot. The shot is effectively silenced, but there is a certain amount of mechanical clatter as the slide moves back and forth and there is the noise of the ejected case hitting the ground. For absolute silence, therefore, a catch on the slide is moved, and this rotates lugs on the breechblock to lock it to the

105. The Chinese Type 67 is an improved Type 64. This picture shows the breechblock withdrawn manually for reloading. By pressing the catch in the recessed upper edge of the block it can either be locked or permitted to reciprocate on firing.

barrel. Now, on firing, the slide does not move and the pistol does not reload; but there is absolutely no noise. Once the assassin has fired he can make his escape and, at some convenient moment, unlock the breech, eject the spent case and reload the pistol.

The Type 64 was later improved into the Type 67; the pistol is mechanically much the same, but the silencer is a rather tidier piece of design, tubular instead of the double-bulbous effect of the original model, which makes the pistol better balanced.

CZECHOSLOVAKIA

Not only did the Czech Army have a bad design of pistol – the self-cocking CZ38 – the exigencies of war had made sure that they got few of them, since the German occupiers took most of the production. So once the country settled down after the war a new pistol was fairly high on the army's agenda. First they had to settle on a cartridge, but before much could be done the country fell under Communist domination and, as is usual with satellites, they had to conform to Soviet standards in weapons and adopt the 7.62mm Mauser cartridge as their service pistol and submachine-gun round.

106. The Czech vz.52 pistol uses a complex and expensive roller-locking system, but has a high reputation for accuracy and long life.

The Czechs, however, are somewhat independent, and while conforming to outward appearance they redesigned the propelling charge and bullet slightly to come up with a cartridge which is rather more powerful than the 7.62mm Soviet – itself a fairly potent round. So from having a weak 9mm Short as their standard in pre-war days, they plunged ahead and adopted a cartridge which would outperform most other pistol rounds.

To fire this, a locked breech was imperative, and it had to be a very sound lock at that. So the CZ52 pistol appeared, with one of the most unusual methods of breech locking ever found on an automatic pistol. The chamber area of the barrel is a block which carries, on its lower edge, two rollers set into recesses. Between these two rollers lies a shaped 'locking cam' which is located firmly in the frame by a lug. The interior of the slide has two semi-circular recesses which match the rollers. When the breech is locked the rollers are partly anchored into the barrel and partly into the slide so that

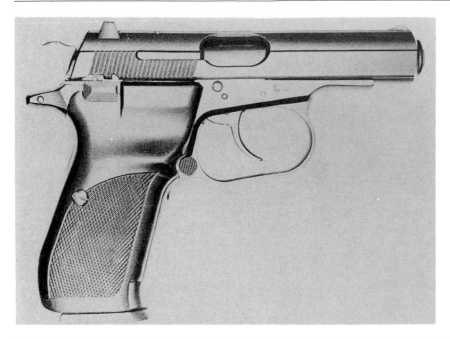

they lock the two together. On firing, the barrel and slide recoil for a short distance, and the rollers are prevented from moving inwards by the edges of the locking cam which lies between them. After the bullet has left the muzzle, the movement of the barrel and slide brings the rollers to the tapered end of the locking cam, and the pressure of the slide can force the rollers inwards so that the slide is now free to continue its rearward movement while the barrel is stopped by a cross-piece on the frame. On the return stroke the slide forces a round into the chamber and begins pushing the barrel forward, but the barrel cannot move because of the rollers, which are pressed inwards by the inside surface of the slide. Eventually the recesses in the slide line up with the rollers and then the shaped end of the locking cam forces the rollers outwards as the barrel moves forward; the rollers enter the recesses in the slide and the breech is locked once more.

This system is very strong and reliable but, as might be imagined, is by no means a cheap method of construction. Nevertheless it remained in service for many years; one advantage of the design is that the barrel does not tilt when unlocking, so very little wear appears in the muzzle bush of the slide and thus it stays very accurate for a long time. In 1983, however,

107. Perhaps because of the complexity of the vz.52, the most recent Czech Army-issue pistol is the CZ83 blowback pictured here.

108. The 9mm Parabellum CZ85 is a high-quality product, but will not appear in Czech military service because it fires a non-Warsaw Pact cartridge.

it began to be replaced by an entirely new weapon, the CZ83. This is a simple blowback design in 7.65mm or 9mm Short calibre, hammer fired with an ambidextrous safety catch and a magazine which holds 15 rounds of 7.65mm ammunition.

Strangely, the best pistol design to appear in Czechoslovakia since the war, the CZ75, was not adopted for military use. This, briefly, is a 9mm Parabellum pistol, double-action, swinging-link lock with a 15-round magazine. Of excellent quality, it is also manufactured under licence in Switzerland and widely exported as a sporting weapon, but there appears to have been no move to adapt it to 7.62mm Soviet calibre for military use.

FRANCE

The French had put their pre-war SACM Modèle 35 back into production as soon as the war was over, but by this time the French Army had realized that their pre-war 7.65mm Longue cartridge was totally unsuited to the realities of

combat and they wanted a pistol chambered for the 9mm Parabellum cartridge. The Manufacture d'Armes de Saint-Etienne soon produced a design which both it and the Manufacture d'Armes de Châtellerault began producing in 1950. The MAS Mle 50 was rather reminiscent of the Saint-Etienne modified Modèle 35S in its slide shape and cross-bolt safety catch, but the butt was larger and rather better-shaped so as to accommodate a magazine holding nine rounds of the larger cartridge. Locking was done by the time-honoured Browning swinging link the patents on which had long expired, and, generally speaking, the French Army at last had a good combat pistol.

In the 1970s, when the fashion for large magazine capacity was beginning, the French Army needed more pistols and turned to private industry. There were few companies left in France capable of making pistols, but the Manufacture d'Armes de Bayonne (MAB), a firm which had been in the pistol business since 1921, had several designs which could be modified to fit the army's requirement. It had, in production for the commercial export market, a design called the 'Modèle R Para' which stemmed from a pre-war model and which was chambered for the 9mm Parabellum cartridge. In other calibres the Model R was a blowback, but the 'R Para' locked the breech by means of a

109. The MAB PA-15, seen here with target sights, has equipped the French Army for a number of years. However, a replacement is currently being sought because of the recent demise of MAB.

rotating barrel. This locked into the slide by a number of lugs and was unlocked by a helical lug underneath the barrel moving through a slot in the frame during recoil. The butt was enlarged to take a 15-shot magazine, and in this form it became the 'Pistolet Automatique 15' or 'MAB PA-15'. A considerable number were issued in the late 1970s, but in the early 1980s the company got into financial difficulties and was wound up. This has left the French Army out on a limb for spares and replacements, and at the time of writing (late 1986) a comparative test is underway to select a new service pistol.

GERMANY (WEST)
The end of the war found Germany's pistol makers in an invidious position; with the exceptin of Mauser, all the rest were in the Russian Zone of Occupation, and their machinery was almost entirely removed to Russia as reparations. Their factories had been damaged by bombing and ground attack, and their stocks had been thoroughly looted by occupying troops, displaced persons and virtually anyone who had a fancy to help himself. In this way the

priceless collections of small arms built up over the years by the major manufacturers were dispersed across the world, the manufacturing base was destroyed and the workforce dispersed. Mauser, being in the French Zone, got off lightly, and was soon put to work by the pragmatic French, manufacturing Parabellum '08 pistols to outfit the French forces. Other manufacturers either stayed in what was now East Germany, to become part of the 'Ernst Thalmann' gunmaking co-operative, or they voted with their feet and fled to the West before the border control got too restrictive. Having done so they had to start from scratch.

Walther had, in addition to firearms, manufactured calculating-machines in the past and now went back into this business with considerable success. It also licensed manufacture of its pre-war pistols to Manurhin of France and Hämmerli of Switzerland.

In the mid 1950s the question of West German participation in the defence of Europe was thrashed out and eventually the Bundeswehr came into being – and needed arms. Its immediate needs were satisfied by American equipment, but the German Army wanted German weapons and, since they could see very little wrong with what they had used prior to 1945, it was to their pre-war designs they turned for pistols and machine-guns. Walther went back into production with the P-38 in 1957, and in 1963 renamed it the P1, having made a change in the material of the frame. In 1968, the frame was strengthened. As well as being adopted by the Bundeswehr, several pre-war German customers also adopted it, including Chile and Portugal, and it is also used by the Norwegian Army.

After Mauser had completed manufacture of Parabellum pistols for the French, the factory was left with nothing very much to do, and many Mauser employees left to seek jobs elsewhere. Among them were two gentlemen named Heckler and Koch, and they decided to set up in the pistol business. Their first product was the HK4, virtually a modernization of the pre-war Mauser HSc insofar as it was a streamlined double-action blowback pistol, though with some unique features. One is the safety system: applying the safety catch merely locks the firing pin, and pulling the trigger then drops the hammer safely so that it can be fired quickly

by merely releasing the safety and pulling the trigger. A principal selling point of the HK4 was that by making a few simple changes the pistol could be adapted to fire .22 Long Rifle rimfire, 6.35mm, 7.65mm or 9mm Short cartridges. A simple change of barrel and magazine sufficed to alter the centre-fire calibres, but the firing pin strike had to be altered by adjusting the breech faceplate in order to fire rimfire cartridges. The HK4 was widely sold commercially and was adopted by some police forces. It remained in production until the early 1980s.

Heckler & Koch's next pistol was the P9, a military-style weapon in 9mm Parabellum chambering. By this time they had begun manufacturing their G3 rifle for the Bundeswehr and other customers, and acquired considerable expertize in a roller-delayed breech locking system which was used in the rifle. This they now applied to their pistol, with considerable success. Although using a similar arrangement of two rollers to lock barrel and slide together, as seen in the Czech CZ52, the H&K system is somewhat more simple in its execution. A two-part breechblock is fitted into the rear of the slide, the rear portion being firmly pinned to the slide, the front section, carrying the face of the breech, being loose. The barrel has a short extension in the form of two arms behind the chamber and these have recesses for the locking rollers. On firing, the front part of the breechblock is forced back by the cartridge in blowback fashion, but it is held by the two rollers which are partly in recesses in the block and partly in the recesses in the barrel extension. But the angles of these recesses are carefully calculated and formed so that the rollers can gradually ease their way out under pressure and thus release the breechblock. Once the rollers are free the loose portion of the block moves back and then thrusts the fixed portion, and hence the slide, to the rear.

The P9 was a shapely, well-manufactured weapon, and despite some misgivings about having a delayed blowback system with 9mm Parabellum, it proved to be reliable and strong. It was adopted by some German police forces and by several military forces in other countries and is still in production. Some early models were made in 7.65mm Parabellum calibre, but this cartridge is now virtually obsolete and the idea was abandoned. More recently it has been made in .45 ACP calibre for sale to the US commercial market.

The P9 was closely followed by a pistol specifically intended for military and para-military use, the VP70. This was a very advanced concept, since it used a great deal of plastic in its construction, could be fitted with a shoulderstock, and was a 9mm Parabellum blowback relying on a strong return spring and a heavy breechblock and slide.

The most unusual feature was the introduction of a three-round burst facility. As a handheld pistol, the VP70 functioned as a conventional semi-automatic; but fitting the shoulderstock automatically operated a link in the pistol's firing mechanism which brought the burst mechanism into play. With this in action every pressure on the trigger gives a burst of three shots. The object of this, which had been pioneered in assault rifles in the late 1960s, was to provide automatic fire without the disadvantage which machine pistols always have, that of the muzzle climb due to recoil forces. An ordinary full-automatic machine pistol fires at a very high rate, due to the low weight of the reciprocating parts and their short stroke, and thus the magazine is emptied in less than a second; it is very difficult to control such fire, and the pistol always climbs out of control, so that the first shot or two may hit the target but the rest are sprayed harmlessly into the air

above it. Proving a three-round burst means that all three rounds are likely to land on or close to the target, but the burst then stops and the firer can get the pistol back under control quickly, take a fresh aim and fire another three rounds.

The VP70 attracted a good deal of attention, but it did not attract many customers. Most were put off by the plain blowback aspect, with such a heavy cartridge, some by the political aspects of arming police with a form of automatic weapon. Some commercial sales were made in Africa and Asia and one or two military and police forces bought them, but the response was not as good as H&K had hoped for and the pistol was taken out of production in the early 1980s.

In the 1970s the German police forces decided it was time they overhauled their armament, largely because of the increase in terrorist crime. A specification was drawn up for what amounted to an ideal pistol and this was circulated to manufacturers; the result was a sudden rejuvenation of pistol design, and not

110. Heckler & Koch's VP70 was innovative in using a large amount of plastic, firing a 9mm Parabellum cartridge (from a blowback pistol) and having a three-round burst capability when the shoulder-stock was attached.

111. The Heckler & Koch P9S pistol uses a two-piece breechblock and rollers to give a very positive delay to the blowback action.

only in Germany. The police were asking for double-action, absolutely foolproof safety and a very fast first-round reaction time. They were also asking for something rather more powerful than the traditional 7.65mm or 9mm Short police cartridge. The responses to this were interesting, and there can be no doubt that this relatively minor request set new standards in pistol design.

The Walther company put forward its P5 Pistol; this was virtually an up-dated and shortened P38, using the same method of locking but with the slide redesigned to cover the barrel and the barrel shortened so that it was barely longer than the frame beneath it. The principal novelty was a total re-arrangement of the firing pin and hammer system so as to fall in line with the police requirement for absolute safety but quick response. The firing pin is held out of alignment with the hammer nose except for the brief period during which the hammer is released by the trigger. Until the instant of hammer release, the firing pin is held down so that its rear end is opposite a recess in the face of the hammer; thus, should the hammer fall, the head of the firing pin will enter the recess and there will be no contact between hammer and pin. There is also a safety notch on the hammer release mechanism. As a result it is impossible for the hammer to strike the firing pin except when the trigger is fully drawn back with the deliberate intention of firing the pistol. No amount of maltreatment, dropping or manipulation of the hammer by itself will cause the pistol to fire.

There is also a de-cocking lever on the left side of the frame, just behind the trigger. Pressing this, when the pistol is loaded and cocked, releases the hammer under control so that it lies with its recess enclosing the end of the firing pin. The firing pin has a lug which engages in a notch in the pin housing so that it cannot move forward or back. On pressing the trigger, the hammer is lifted and, just before the hammer is released, the firing pin is also lifted so that the lug is clear of the notch and the pin is lined up with the solid face of the hammer.

112. The Heckler & Koch P7 uses an unusual form of gas delay, and also cocks the pistol only when the grip-cocking device in the front of the butt is squeezed.

The P5 was well-received, and was adopted by the police forces of two German provinces and by The Netherlands police. It has also been taken into service as a military pistol in Portugal, Nigeria and some South American countries.

The Heckler & Koch offering was a totally new pistol which introduced some new concepts. Chambered for the 9mm Parabellum, the PSP (later re-named the P7), used a system of gas delayed blowback operation which was quite unique. Beneath the fixed barrel is a cylinder which is connected to the barrel by a small gas port. At the front end of the slide is attached a piston rod which fits inside this cylinder. The return spring is wrapped around the barrel, and there is a secondary spring around the gas piston rod. On firing, the cylinder fills with high-pressure gas, tapped from the gases following the bullet, and this high pressure acts to resist the inward movement of the piston rod due to the recoil of the slide. Once the bullet has left the barrel, the piston rod can force the gas back through the port and exhaust it through the barrel, but the amount of delay is sufficient to make the pistol safe to operate.

The firing mechanism is also unusual. Instead of the usual hammer there is a firing pin carried in the rear of the slide, but the forward movement of the slide, re-loading the chamber, does not cock the firing pin. Instead, cocking is performed manually by the firer when he grips the pistol; there is a squeeze-grip in the front surface of the butt, and as this is squeezed by the firer in the act of holding the pistol firmly, so it cocks the firing pin. The pistol is then fired by pulling the trigger in the usual way, and so long as the squeeze grip is kept pressed, the pistol will re-cock after each shot. As soon as pressure on the grip is relaxed, so the firing pin is uncocked; if the firer were to drop the pistol it would immediately go to a safe condition before it even hit the ground.

The squeeze grip also functions as a slide release; after the last shot in the magazine has been fired, the slide remains open. After putting a new magazine in place, a squeeze of the grip releases the slide to chamber a fresh round and cock the firing pin.

The P7 first appeared in two models, the P7M8 and the P7M13, the difference being solely one of magazine capacity, the last figure in the designation showing how many rounds were in the magazine. It has since been supplemented by the P7K3 which is in 9mm Short calibre and dispenses with the gas delay system. This has a magazine capacity of eight rounds and is replacing the HK4 as the 'pocket pistol' of the Heckler & Koch range.

In 1986 the company introduced the P7M7, in .45ACP calibre with a 7-shot magazine. This changes the operating system slightly by using a cylinder of oil in place of the gas cylinder of the P7. On firing, the rearward movement of the slide forces a piston rod into the oil cylinder; since oil is incompressible, it has to escape somewhere in order to admit the piston rod, and it is forced through a valve in the piston-head so as to pass into the front end of the cylinder, the effort of forcing the oil through the valve serving to brake the movement of the slide. On the return stroke the oil flows the other way through a larger valve so as not to slow up the closing stroke of the slide. The whole system is very much akin to the oil buffer used with artillery guns. The result is that it soaks up a large amount of the recoil force and makes the P7M7 one of the more pleasant and controllable .45 pistols.

The various P7 designs have been enormously successful and have been taken into service by many police and military forces throughout the world.

It is worth noting that the Mauser company also produced a prototype pistol for the police trials; this was the HsP, a double-action design in 9mm Parabellum calibre with a de-cocking lever. It did not do well in its trials, and Mauser decided that there was little point in continuing with pistol production. They had already licensed production of their HsC pistol to an Italian company, and they had spent some time producing the Parabellum pistol once more, largely to satisfy collectors, but their business was now more in the heavy weapons field and their share of the pistol market was not worth a major investment in design and development.

GREAT BRITAIN

When Belgium was overrun in 1940 several members of the staff of FN managed to escape to Britain. Although there is little or no documentary evidence, it seems that the drawings of

the GP-35 were brought with them and that a small number were manufactured in Britain in 1941 as the 'Pistol, Browning, 9mm (FN) Automatic Mark I (UK)' since there is a record of its approval being cancelled in April 1945 in a general clearance of obsolete wartime designs, but there is no record of its ever being formally introduced into service. In 1942, however, the drawings were sent to Canada and the John Inglis company of Toronto manufactured it for supply to the Chinese Nationalist Army. It was then adopted, in small numbers, by the British and Canadian armies, principally for use by Airborne and Commando units. Four models were made: the 'Pistol, Browning FN 9mm No 1 Mark I' had the adjustable rear sight and a shoulder-stock; 'No 1 Mark I*' was the same, but with an improved ejector and sight; 'No 2 Mark I' had the fixed rear sight and no stock; and 'No 2 Mark I*' was as No 2 Mark I but with the improved ejector. With the end of the war came the end of Inglis' production, and manufacture reverted to the FN factory in Liège.

By the mid 1950s the British stock of revolvers was getting low, and their experience with the wartime Brownings having been satisfactory, after a short period of tests with pistols of the latest pattern from FN the British Army finally succumbed to the relentless pressure of progress and in 1957 formally adopted the FN Browning GP-35 as their standard pistol. The model adopted was the 'No 2 Mark I' pattern as

113. The Mo.951 was Beretta's first locked breech pistol, though it retains the characteristic open-top slide.

improved by FN, and it has remained the British service pistol ever since.

ITALY

The Beretta Model 34 in 9mm Short had served the Italian Army well throughout the war and, into the bargain, had become one of the more esteemed souvenirs for Allied troops on the Italian front. But 9mm Short no longer seemed to be the preferred calibre, and Beretta began studying a locked-breech design to fire the 9mm Parabellum cartridge. They retained the open-topped slide which, by now, had become almost a Beretta trademark, and adopted a locking system which was very similar to that used by the Walther P-38, a wedge beneath the barrel which locked it to the slide at the time of firing but then was withdrawn by a ramp after a short recoil. The design was patented in 1950, but the pistol did not go into full production until 1957, because the original design called for a light alloy frame in order to reduce the weight. This, though, appears to have produced a pistol which was neither accurate nor pleasant to shoot, and the design was reworked to use a steel frame.

The Beretta M951, as the production pistol is called, was almost immediately adopted by the Italian Army, and shortly afterwards was also

114. The Beretta Mo.951R is a modification of the 951 with an additional front grip and the capacity for automatic fire.

115. The Beretta 93R, a variation of the 951, popular with the Italian special forces, has a front grip, a shoulder-stock and an ability to fire three-round bursts.

taken into use by Egypt, Israel and some other Middle Eastern countries. In addition, a special Model 951A was developed for use by the Carabinieri; this has a folding, front pistol grip on the frame and a 125mm barrel, and can be switched to give full-automatic fire.

Beretta then spent the next few years perfecting a series of small-calibre blowback double-action pistols for the commercial and police markets and in 1976 introduced the military member of this family, the Model 92. This was in 9mm Parabellum, used the same locking wedge as did their earlier M951, had a double-action lock with external hammer, and had a firing pin which was firmly locked except during the final stroke of the trigger as the hammer reached full-cock. The Model 92 was taken into service by the Italian Army and, made by Forjas Taurus, has been adopted in Brazil.

In the early 1980s the design was modified into the Model 92S; this was more or less the same, but moved the safety catch from the frame to the rear of the slide and introduced a de-cocking function. Pressing the safety catch now moves the firing pin into a safe position

and locks it there, then releases the hammer and breaks the connection between trigger and hammer.

Shortly after this, the United States Army began trials to select a new service pistol to replace the Colt M1911A1 model. The ups and downs of this trial are too long and involved to describe here; Beretta, however, put the Model 92S forward, modified to suit the American requirements. The principal changes were simply the provision of an ambidextrous safety catch and the positioning of the magazine release in the forward edge of the butt (American practice) rather than in the heel of the butt (European practice). This revised model was called the Model 92SB, and it was accompanied by a 'compact' version, the 92SB-C, which was slightly smaller and had a 13-shot magazine instead of the SB's 15-shot magazine.

After many months of trials and arguments, the US Army finally settled on a slightly changed version of the SB as their future pistol. This was the Model 92F and it differed from the SB in having the forward edge of the trigger guard shaped to suit a two-handed grip, in having an extended base to the magazine to give a greater grip surface, new grip plates, a new lanyard ring, an internally-chromed barrel and a 'Bruniton' corrosion-resistant finish. In early 1985 it was announced that this would become the new standard US sidearm for use

116. The Beretta 92F was recently adopted as the 9mm Pistol M9 by the US Army, though the decision may yet be rescinded.

by all military forces, under the designation M9.

In order to cater for all possible tastes, Beretta have continued to develop minor variants of the Model 92 family. The Model 92SB-C Type M is the same as the SB-C, but has an 8-shot magazine; the 92F Compact is the same as the 92SB-C but has the various modifications which changed the 92SB into the 92F; the Model 98 is the 92SB-C chambered for the 7.65mm Parabellum cartridge; and the Model 98F is the 92F chambered for 7.65mm Parabellum.

POLAND
One might reasonably have expected the Poles to put the 9mm Radom back into production once the war was over, but this did not happen. Instead, the country went into the Soviet Bloc and as a result was required to conform to Soviet standards, which meant adopting the Tokarev TT33 pistol. In the 1960s, when the

Soviets moved to blowback weapons, the Poles followed suit and adopted the PM-64. This bears some external resemblance to the Makarov, and much internal resemblance to the Walther PP, being a fixed-barrel blowback pistol with double-action lock. It is chambered for the 9 × 19mm Soviet Makarov cartridge.

SPAIN
When the Civil War ended in 1939, legislation brought an end to the free-for-all era of Spanish gunmaking, and only three companies, Astra, Llama and Star, were permitted to manufacture pistols. Astra continued to make its Model 400 service pistol and its derivatives, and later went into the manufacture of small-calibre blowback pocket automatics and revolvers. Llama and Star based their automatic pistol designs largely on the well-tried Colt M1911 system. Their pistols generally copied the outline and, if in large calibre, used the swinging link locking system; if small calibre, they were often blowbacks, though even 9mm Short designs some-

117. The Star Mo.28 DA, adopted by the Spanish Army.

times used the full locking system, for no apparently good reason. It was not until the late 1970s that any Spanish manufacturer was moved to produce something new; by that time the spate of new designs appearing in Germany, Italy and Switzerland were making themselves felt on the world markets, and it became obvious that unless Spain produced something more in line with modern requirements their pistol sales would decline drastically.

The Star company (Bonifacio Echeverria of Eibar) were the first to respond, with their Model 28DA pistol. This uses the familiar cam action to unlock the barrel from the slide, much as the Browning GP-35 or SIG designs, has double-action lockwork with an external hammer, and a 15-shot magazine. In 9mm Parabellum calibre, it is also unusual in that it adopts the SIG system of supporting the slide in internal frame rails, giving a minimum bearing

surface of 110mm and maximum support throughout the recoil movement. There is an ambidextrous safety catch on the slide which retracts the safety pin and locks it so that it cannot be struck by the hammer. The trigger and hammer action are quite unaffected by the operation of this safety lever, so that it is possible to pull the trigger after applying the safety in order to drop the hammer, and it is also possible to 'dry fire' the pistol for practise without needing to unload and without placing any strain on the firing pin. Whether this is a good thing is a matter for discussion; it seems possible that one could absent-mindedly draw the pistol set at safe and pull through on the trigger expecting to fire a shot and be rewarded with a click, which could be embarrassing in some situations.

The Star offering was followed in 1982 by the Astra A-80. This is very similar in concept, a 9mm Parabellum pistol, double-action, with automatic firing pin safety and a de-cocking lever. In fact, and not to put too fine a point on

118. The Astra A-90, another modern design that has been purchased by the Spanish armed forces.

it, the Astra A-80 has obviously been designed with one eye on the SIG P220.

Astra followed the A-80 with the A-90, announced in 1985. This adds to the system a slide-mounted safety catch which, when rotated, moves a section of the two-piece firing pin out of the path of the hammer. This is in addition to the existing automatic safety which prevents movement of the front part of the firing pin except when the trigger is fully pressed. The A-90 is available in 9mm Parabellum with a 15-round magazine or in .45 ACP with an 8-round magazine.

SWEDEN

In 1939 Sweden was in the process of adopting the Walther Heeres-Pistole as their standard military pistol, but before they had received very many of them the war intervened and, the source of supply being otherwise engaged,

deliveries stopped. They therefore turned to Finland and obtained a licence to manufacture the Lahti, taking it into service as the 9mm Model 40. According to some authorities the Swedish pistol was not quite as good as the Finnish model, largely because the Swedes were unable to obtain precisely the right grades of steel for some of the components, but this appears to have been overcome and the final production models leave little to be desired.

However, the Swedish Army introduced a 'hot' 9mm cartridge for use in submachine-guns; it was a 9mm Parabellum round but of rather more power than usual, and after some years of using this in pistols it was found that frames were cracking. The Lahti was, therefore, retired in 1983 and the venerable Browning M1907 (Mle 1903) in 9mm Browning Long calibre has been resurrected as the standard Swedish Army pistol. This had been manu-factured under licence in Sweden from 1908 to 1943, so that there were ample stocks held in reserve. Which gives Sweden the dubious distinction of having the oldest first-line service weapon in the world. It is understood that the Swedish Army have been holding comparative trials of modern pistols to seek a replacement, but, at the time of writing, these have been shelved because of financial restrictions on new procurement.

SWITZERLAND

The only people who were at all interested in pistol development during the war years were the Swiss, who, of course, were neutral. Even so, they were well aware that Germany periodically drew up plans for invading Switzerland, and they were a well-prepared neutral by the time the war ended. The SIG company had, some time prior to the war, looked ahead and envisaged a time when the 7.65mm Parabellum would no longer be acceptable as a military pistol, and was determined to have a design ready against that day. For this reason it had bought the Petter patents, as previously related, and quietly fiddled about with this throughout the war years, altering, perfecting and polishing the design. At the same time, the National Arsenal at Berne was also working on a design, but this establishment suffered from the presence of their chief designer, Colonel Adolf Furrer, a genius who would never suffer a simple design if a complicated one were available, so the Berne pistols were gas-operated masterpieces of complexity with little real hope of success.

In 1944 SIG produced a small number of pistols called the 'Neuhausen 44/16' – from the name of the town in which SIG had its factory, the year, and the 16-round capacity of the magazine – and the 'Neuhausen 44/8' (which held eight shots). The army failed to respond in any positive manner, so SIG continued to make small improvements and in 1948 placed the design on the market as the SP 47/8 in 9mm Parabellum calibre, with the possibility of changing barrel and magazine to convert it to 7.65mm Parabellum when required.

The SP 47/8 was a locked breech pistol which had come a long way since Petter last saw it. The swinging link method of unlocking was abandoned for a fixed steel lug beneath the breech with a curved slot cut in it, through which passed a frame pin. Thus on recoil the

slot was driven across the pin and this withdrew the barrel lugs from the slide. The hammer, sear and other lock components were carried in a removable 'action casing'. The most unusual feature was that the slide was riding on rails inside the frame, instead of outside, which every other slide-pattern automatic pistol had done. It was more expensive and difficult to manufacture, but it gave much better support to the slide during the recoil movement. Another innovation was to do away with the usual muzzle bush which centred the barrel in the front of the slide; instead, the hole in the slide was extremely precisely contoured so that it always gave firm support to the barrel, irrespective of what angle it was at, and there was no loose movement at any time. The barrel actually does not leave the horizontal until the bullet is well clear of the muzzle, and the combination of muzzle location and interior slide rails gives this pistol a degree of inherent accuracy not found on any other comparable weapon.

The SP47/8 in 9mm Parabellum was adopted by the Swiss Army in October 1948 as the 'Ordonnanzpistole 49'; shortly afterwards the West German Border Police adopted it, and then the Danish Army. Since that time it has been taken into service by one or two smaller African nations, but the truth of the matter is that, while it is undoubtedly an excellent pistol, it is equally certainly an expensive one, and one which, for that reason, is never likely to be adopted in large numbers. But as long as there are competition shooters who require a carefully made and accurate pistol, SIG will continue to make and sell the P-210, as it is commercially known.

In the 1960s the Swiss passed a series of laws which severely restricted the sales of arms to foreign countries; in the words of one Swiss manufacturer, 'We are only permitted to sell arms to people who don't need them.' This struck particularly hard on small arms, and the SIG company therefore entered into an agreement with the J. P. Sauer company of Germany, under which SIG would design weapons but Sauer would manufacture and market them. This stratagem opened up markets which the Swiss could never otherwise reach and it has given rise to a series of excellent 'SIG-Sauer' pistols. Although manufactured in West

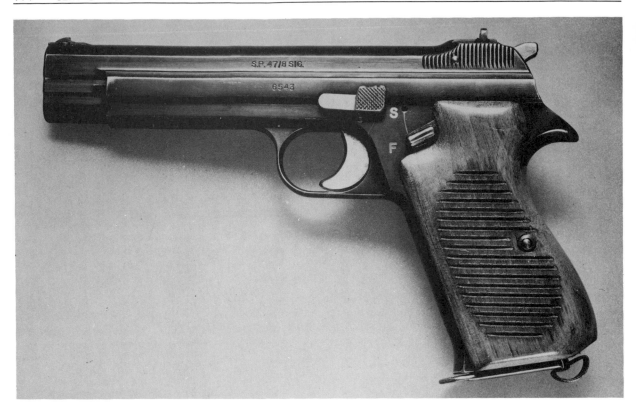

119. The SIG P-210, judged by some to be the best automatic pistol in the world. It has been used by the Swiss and Danish armies, as well as by German border guards and many police units.

120, 121. Two newer SIG-designed pistols, made in Germany by Sauer & Sohn, are the tipping-barrel P220 (120, 121 top) and the P230 blowback (121 bottom).

Germany they will be considered here, since they form the continuation of SIG development.

The first SIG-Sauer model to appear was the P-220. This introduced the new SIG locking system which is the Browning cam taken to its ultimate: the barrel has a lug beneath the chamber which is shaped to engage with a transom in the slide and so pull the rear end of the barrel down on recoil. The chamber section of the barrel is formed externally into a squared-off lump with well-defined shoulders at the front, and this is lifted by the cam so that it locks into the ejection port in the slide. The ejection port is set squarely in the centre of the slide, and not off to the side as had formerly been the normal practice. The pistol is hammer-fired and double-action, and there is a de-cocking lever on the left side which is very reminiscent of the Sauer Model 38; so much so that it is generally considered that Sauer engineers had a hand in the design, though the designers and manufacturers will not comment on this. The firing pin is locked by a spring-loaded plunger which passes through a hole in the pin; this is only disengaged when the trigger is pulled back and the hammer is on the point of release, so that the pistol is quite safe unless intentionally operated. There is no manual safety device.

The P-220 was adopted by the Swiss as their Pistole 75 and has now almost entirely replaced the P210 and Parabellum models. It is manufactured under licence in Japan and is the standard issue pistol of the Japanese Self-Defence Force. It is currently under evaluation by other armies and may well be adopted in Sweden in the 1990s.

The P-225 is a slightly improved version of the P-220: it is slightly smaller and lighter, and the magazine carries eight rounds of 9mm Parabellum instead of nine. There are some very small differences in contours and in details of the safety system. The P-225 was adopted as standard by the Swiss Federal Police and by several German police forces.

The P-226 was developed by SIG in 1980 as their entrant for the US Army pistol contest, in which it very nearly succeeded, failing only on the grounds of price. About 80 per cent of its component parts came from the P-220 and P-225, the only differences being in the provision of an ambidextrous magazine catch and a 15-round magazine. SIG considers this to be the best pistol it has ever designed, an opinion with which it is hard to argue, and although details are not disclosed by the company it is believed that the P-226 is now in use by many important security agencies throughout the world.

USA

Apart from some small modifications to the Colt M1911 in 1926, which turned it into the M1911A1, the US services had retained the same .45 automatic since 1911, and by the mid 1970s there were those who freely prophesied that the venerable Colt would become the first 100-year-old weapon. They were to be proved wrong.

There was, and is to this day, a considerable body of opinion in the USA which maintained that nothing smaller than .45 calibre should ever be contemplated for military service, but the trend of world opinion was against them. 9mm Parabellum had become virtually the world standard for pistols and submachine-guns, outside the Warsaw Pact that is, and since the USA was the principal partner in NATO it was obvious that, sooner or later, it would have to conform to NATO standardization and adopt 9mm as their service calibre. In the late 1970s a programme of tests was set in motion to determine which pistol would replace the Colt.

As has been mentioned previously, this turned out to be a traumatic affair, larded with political overtones, and the lawsuits are by no means over yet. The eventual choice was the Beretta Model 92F, described above, but there are still attempts being made to overturn this decision in favour of an American weapon.

Without going into the test results and conclusions, it can be said that there is only one viable contender from inside the USA and that is the Smith & Wesson Model 459, a double-action 9mm pistol with a 14-round magazine. This is a first-class weapon which has met with commercial success. It led to the Model 469, a compact version, developed to meet a specification issued by the US Air Force; this is somewhat smaller in all dimensions, has a hammer without spur, and uses a 12-shot magazine. Both these models use the cam system to unlock barrel and slide.

122. The Smith & Wesson 459, a 9mm pistol of high quality, was strongly favoured for adoption by the US armed forces, only to be pipped at the post by the Beretta 92F.

USSR

The Tokarev TT-33 remained the standard service pistol in the Soviet Army for many years, and numbers are held in reserve and second-line formations. In the early 1950s, however, a new pistol made its appearance and began replacing the Tokarev. This was the 'PM' or Makarov, broadly a copy of the Walther PP and chambered for a totally new cartridge. The 9mm Makarov round is slightly smaller than the 9mm Parabellum, larger than the 9mm Short, and thus is perhaps the most powerful round that can safely be used with a blowback pistol. Although there are slight differences in contour here and there, the operation of the Makarov is exactly the same as that of the Walther, with a double-action lock and a slide-mounted safety which locks the firing pin and drops the hammer when applied. The grip is somewhat bulky, though the magazine holds only eight rounds, and the pistol appears to be well made, of good materials. It has been widely adopted in other Warsaw Pact armies and has been manufactured in China and other satellite countries.

Shortly after the appearance of the Makarov, the 'APS' (Stechkin) pistol was revealed. This was a much larger and heavier pistol, even though it fired the same 9mm Makarov cartridge, and the reason for its bulk was simply to absorb as much recoil as possible, since the Stechkin was a machine pistol; it could be switched to fire full automatic at a rate of 750 rounds per minute. Mechanically it is still a blowback, but has a selector which permits single shots or automatic fire, and the butt is slotted to take a short stock, which is necessary for automatic shooting. Held in the hand it would be quite uncontrollable at such a high rate of fire.

The Stechkin was issued as an infantry section weapon for some years, but in the late 1970s it began to fade from the scene, probably because it was realized that it was not a practical device and was merely wasting ammunition. So far as we are aware it has been entirely removed from Soviet Army units, but doubtless several thousands remain in reserve

and it is likely to be passed to satellite nations and 'Liberation Movements' at any time.

In 1983 came the news of yet another pistol for Soviet military use, this one apparently reserved for security forces and military police. This is the PSM pistol, a commonplace blowback but in a very odd calibre. It fires a 5.45mm bottlenecked cartridge of low power, a design which is unique to this pistol and which appears to have no technical justification whatsoever; the pistol could equally well have been chambered for 6.35mm or 7.65mm ACP without changing the dimensions. The PSM pistol resembles the Walther PP in general appearance, dimensions and mechanical arrangements, except that the safety catch protrudes from the rear of the slide, alongside the hammer; it is presumed that this position has been chosen in order to make the pistol as slim as possible for concealed carrying.

YUGOSLAVIA

The Yugoslavs inhabit a peculiar position, tied to the Communist philosophy but not to the Warsaw Pact, and therefore have developed some individuality in weapons. Their major

123. The Soviet Army uses the Makarov pistol, here seen in its East German-made form.

military designs are generally based on Soviet originals – the Simonov and Kalashnikov rifles for example – and their standard sidearm was originally the 7.62mm M57 pistol, a Yugoslav-made version of the Tokarev TT-33. Mechanically identical, it can be distinguished from the Soviet model only by its markings. However, some originality crept in with the Model 70(d) which is the same pistol, but chambered for the 9mm Parabellum cartridge. This makes a rather more practical weapon, though the 9mm bullet has less penetrative power than has the 7.62mm bullet.

In the 1970s two blowback pistols entered service and are now widely distributed throughout Yugoslav military and para-military forces. These are the 7.65mm Model 70, firing the commercial 7.65mm ACP cartridge, and the 9mm Model 70(k) firing the 9mm Short cartridge. Both are hammer-fired conventional designs, somewhat bulky for their calibres but certainly sufficiently robust to withstand military employment.

APPENDIX 1
SERVICE PISTOLS OF THE MAJOR NATIONS

Because of lack of information for some key periods, some of the dates should be considered approximate. Unless stated otherwise, all gun designations are the same as the years of adoption.

Argentina
1905: Mannlicher 7.65mm pistol
1916: Colt M1911 .45 pistol
1927: Colt M1911A1 .45 pistol
1936: Ballester-Molina .45 pistol
1955: FN-Browning High Power 9mm pistol

Austria
1952: Walther 9mm P38 pistol
1984: Glock M17 9mm pistol

Austria-Hungary
1873: Gasser-Kropatschek 9mm officers' revolver
1877: Smith & Wesson 11mm troopers' revolver
1880: Gasser 11mm troopers' revolver
1898: Rast & Gasser 8mm infantry revolver
1907: Roth-Steyr 8mm pistol
1912: Frommer 7.65mm pistol (Honved only)
1914: Steyr 9mm pistol M1912

Belgium
1871: Chamelot-Delvigne 11mm troopers' revolver
1878: Nagant 9mm officers' revolver
1883: Nagant 9mm troopers' revolver
1886: Nagant 9mm officers' revolver
1900: FN-Browning 7.65mm 'Old Model' pistol
1903: FN-Browning 9mm pistol
1922: FN-Browning 9mm pistol
1935: FN-Browning High Power 9mm pistol

Brazil
1883: Nagant 9mm troopers' revolver
1886: Nagant .44 cavalry revolver
1908: Parabellum 7.65mm pistol
1920: Mauser 7.63mm pistol
1940: Colt M1911A1 .45 pistol
1973: M973 .45 pistol (Colt copy)
1983: Beretta M92 (Taurus made) 9mm pistol

China
1905: Mauser 7.63mm pistol
1906: FN-Browning 'Old Model' 7.65mm pistol
1942: FN-Browning High Power 9mm pistol (originally Inglis-made)

China, People's Republic
1951: Type 51 7.62mm pistol (Tokarev copy)
1964: Type 64 7.65mm silenced pistol
1977: Type 77 7.62mm pistol
1983: Type 59 9mm pistol (Makarov copy)

China, Republic of (Taiwan)
1950: FN-Browning High Power 9mm pistol
1950: Colt M1911A1 .45 pistol

Denmark
1861: Christensen (Lefaucheux) pinfire navy revolver
1865: Christensen (Lefaucheux) pinfire troopers' revolver
1882: Lefaucheux-Francotte 11mm troopers' revolver
1886: Lefaucheux-Francotte 9mm officers' revolver
1891: Rongé 9mm navy revolver
1910: Bergmann-Bayard 9mm pistol
1950: SIG P210 9mm pistol
1975: SIG-Sauer P220 9mm pistol

Finland
1919: Ruby 7.65mm pistol
1923: Parabellum 7.65mm pistol
1935: Lahti 9mm pistol

France
1856: Lefaucheux 11mm pinfire navy revolver
1858: modified Lefaucheux 11mm pinfire navy revolver
1870: Lefaucheux 11mm rimfire navy revolver
1873: Chamelot-Delvigne 11mm troopers' revolver
1874: Chamelot-Delvigne 11mm officers' revolver
1892: Lebel ('Modèle d'Ordonnance') 8mm revolver
1915: Ruby 7.65mm pistol (war service)

1935: SACM 7.65mm pistol
1950: MAS 9mm pistol
1975: MAB PA-15 9mm pistol

Germany
1879: Reichsrevolver 10.6mm troopers' (or cavalry) model
1883: Reichsrevolver 10.6mm officers' (or infantry) model
1904: Parabellum 9mm navy pistol (Selbstladepistole 1904)
1908: Parabellum 9mm army pistol (Pistole 1908)
1913: Parabellum 9mm army pistol (lang Pistole 08 or 'artillery' model)
1915: Mauser C/96 pistol (war service)
1915: Beholla pistol 7.65mm (war service)
1915: Langenhan pistol 7.65mm (war service)
1915: Dreyse pistol 7.65mm (war service)
1915: Walther pistol 7.65mm (war service)
1916: Steyr pistol 9mm (war service, Bavaria only)
1940: Walther pistol 9mm (Pistole 38)
1940: Walther PP and PPK, 7.65mm and 9mm (war service)
1940: Mauser HSc, 7.65mm and 9mm (war service)
1940: Sauer 38H, 7.65mm and 9mm (war service)
1952: SIG P210 (federal border guards)
1957: Walther P-38 9mm (later 'P1')
1975: Walther P5 9mm (police)
1975: SIG-Sauer P6 (P226, police)
1975: Heckler & Koch P7 (PSP, police)
1980: Heckler & Koch Pistole 7 9mm (armed forces)

Germany, Democratic Republic
1960: Pistole M 9mm (Makarov copy)

Great Britain and Commonwealth
1880: Enfield .476 revolver Mark I
1882: Enfield .476 revolver Mark II
1887: Webley .476 revolver Mark I
1894: Webley .442 revolver Mark II
1897: Webley .455 revolver Mark III
1899: Webley .455 revolver Mark IV

1912: Webley .455 pistol Mark I
1913: Webley .455 revolver Mark V
1915: Webley .455 revolver Mark VI
1915: Colt M1911 .455 pistol
(war service)
1915: Garate, Anitua, Pistol OP No. 1
(revolver, war service)
1915: Trocaola, Aranzabal, Pistol OP
No. 2 (revolver, war service)
1932: Enfield .38 revolver No. 1 Mk I
1938: Enfield .38 revolver No. 1 Mk I*
1940: Smith & Wesson .38/200
revolver (war service)
1954: FN-Browning High Power 9mm
pistol

Hungary
1929: Frommer 29M 7.65mm pistol
1937: Frommer 37M 9mm pistol
1948: Walam 48M 7.65mm pistol
(Walther PP copy)

Israel
1948: Smith & Wesson-type 9mm
revolver
1953: Beretta M951 9mm pistol

Italy
1858: Lefaucheux pinfire revolver,
navy
1872: Chamelot-Delvigne 10.4mm
troopers' revolver
1879: Chamelot-Devigne 10.4mm
officers' revolver
1889: Bodeo 10.4mm revolver
general issue
1899: Mauser C/96 7.63mm pistol
(navy)
1910: Glisenti 9mm pistol
1915: Beretta 7.65mm pistol
1931: Beretta 9mm pistol (navy only)
1934: Beretta 9mm pistol
1935: Beretta 7.65mm pistol (airforce
only)
1957: Beretta Mo.951 9mm pistol
1976: Beretta Mo.93R 9mm machine
pistol (principally for
Carabinieri)
1982: Beretta Mo.92 9mm pistol

Japan
1880: Smith & Wesson .44 Russian
revolver
1893: Type 26 9mm revolver
1915: Nambu 4th Year Type 8mm
pistol
1926: Nambu 14th Year Type 8mm
pistol
1937: Type 94 8mm pistol
1957: Type 57A New Nambu pistol
1982: SIG-Sauer P220 9mm pistol

Mexico
1925: Colt .45 M1911 pistol
1938: Obregon .45 pistol

The Netherlands
1873: Chamelot-Delvigne 9.4mm
revolver
1891: Colonial revolver 9.4mm
(Netherlands Indies Army only)
1911: Parabellum 9mm pistol
(Netherlands Indies Army only)
1925: FN-Browning Mle 10/22 9mm
pistol
1947: FN-Browning High Power 9mm
pistol

Norway
1864: Lefaucheux 11mm pinfire
troopers' revolver
1864: Lefaucheux 11mm pinfire
officers' revolver
1883: 9mm Nagant revolver (general
issue)
1893: 7.5mm Nagant revolver
(general issue)
1912 Colt M1911 .45 pistol (made at
Königsberg as m/1914)

Poland
1928: wz/1928 pistol (Czech vz.24)
1929: Nagant 7.62mm 'gas-seal'
revolver
1935: wz/1935 9mm pistol (Radom or
VIS-35)
1964: P-64 9mm pistol
1970: Makarov 9mm pistol

Portugal
1878: Abadie 9.1mm officers' revolver
1886: Abadie 9.1mm troopers'
revolver
1909: Parabellum 7.65mm pistol
(army)
1910: Parabellum 9mm pistol (navy)
1915: Savage 7.65mm pistol
1935: Parabellum 7.65mm pistol
(GNR only)
1943: Parabellum 9mm pistol
1960: Walther P38 (P1) 9mm pistol
1975: Walther P5 pistol

Romania
1876: Buescu 9mm officers' revolver
1895: Nagant 8mm revolver (general
issue)
1896: Lebel Mle 92 8mm revolver
1912: Steyr-Hahn 9mm pistol
1950: Tokarev 7.62mm pistol

Spain
1858: Lefaucheux 11mm pinfire
troopers' revolver
1863: Lefaucheux 11mm pinfire

troopers' revolver
1885: Smith & Wesson 11mm .44
Russian, officers' revolver
1905: Bergmann-'Mars' 9mm pistol
1908: Bergmann-Bayard 9mm pistol
1914: Mo.1913 Campo-Giro 9mm
pistol
1916: Mo.1913–16 Campo-Giro 9mm
pistol
1921: Astra 9mm pistol (Mo.400)
1922: Star Modelo B 9mm pistol
(Guardia Civil)
1928: Astra 9mm pistol (Mo.300,
navy)
1939: Star Modelo B 9mm pistol
1982: Star Modelo 28DA 9mm pistol
1985: Astra A-80 9mm pistol

Sweden
1865: Lefaucheux-Francotte 11mm
pinfire artillery revolver
1871: Lefaucheux-Francotte 11mm
troopers' revolver
1887: 7.5m Nagant officers' revolver
1907: FN-Browning Mle 1903 9mm
pistol
1939: Walther 9mm HP
1940: Lahti 9mm pistol (made by
Husqvarna)
1985: FN-Browning Mle 1903
reintroduced

Switzerland
1872: Chamelot-Delvigne 10.4mm
rimfire troopers' revolver
1878: Schmidt 10.4mm centrefire
troopers' revolver
1882: Ordonnanzrevolver 1882
7.5mm (Schmidt)
1900: Ordonnanzpistole 1900 7.65mm
(Parabellum)
1906: Ordonnanzpistole 1906 7.65mm
(Parabellum)
1929: Ordonnanzrevolver 82/29
7.5mm
1929: Ordonnanzpistole 06/29
7.65mm W+F (Parabellum)
1948: Ordonnanzpistole 49 9mm
(SIG)
1978: Ordonnanzpistole 75 9mm
(SIG-Sauer P220)

USSR/Russia
1878: Smith & Wesson .44 Russian
revolver
1895: Nagant 7.62mm 'gas-seal'
revolver
1920: Mauser C/96 7.63mm pistol
(semi-official)
1928: Tula-Korovin 6.35mm pistol
(TK)
1930: Tokarev 7.62mm pistol (TT-30)
1933: modified Tokarev pistol (TT-33)

1960: Makarov 9mm pistol (PM)
1962: Stechkin 9mm machine pistol (APS)
1983: PSM 5.45mm pistol

USA
1873: Colt .45 Single Action Army revolver

1874: Smith & Wesson .45 Schofield revolver
1878: Colt .45 Double-Action Army revolver
1892: Colt .38 New Army revolver
1899: Smith & Wesson .38 Hand Ejector revolver
1911: Colt-Browning .45 M1911 pistol

1917: Colt .45 M1917 revolver
1917: Smith & Wesson .45 M1917 revolver
1926: Colt-Browning .45 M1911A1 pistol
1972: Colt .45 General Officers' Pistol
1985: M9 9mm pistol (Beretta 92F)

THE MAUSER ZIG-ZAG REVOLVER

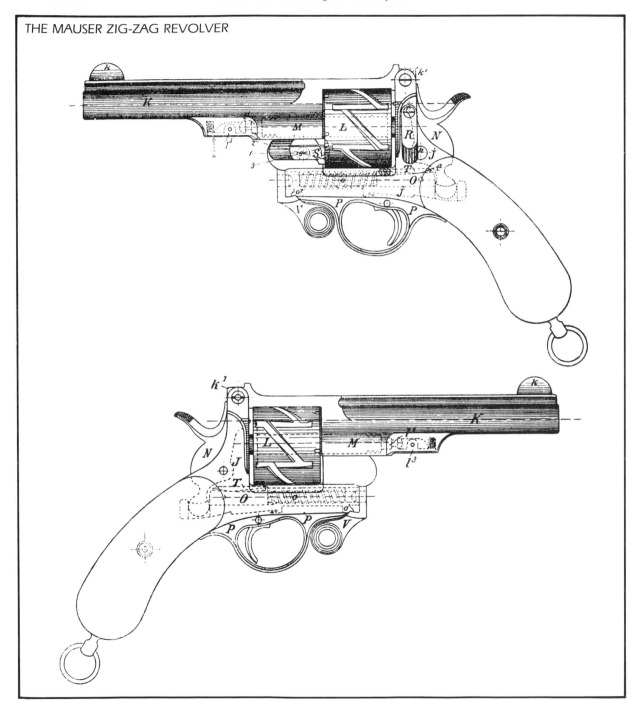

APPENDIX 2
DATA OF THE WORLD'S PRINCIPAL PISTOLS

Name	Calibre	Cartridge	Overall length (mm)	Barrel length (mm)	Rifling grooves	Rifling twist	Weight empty (gm)	Magazine capacity	Muzzle velocity (m/sec)
Argentina									
Mannlicher	7.63mm	7.63 Mann	246	157	4	R	910	8	315
Ballester-Molina	.45	.45 ACP	228	127	6	R	1130	7	265
Austria									
Steyr GB	9mm	9 Para	216	136	4 Poly	R	845	18	ca 375
Glock 17	9mm	9 Para	188	114	6 Poly	R	620	17	ca 350
Austro-Hungarian Empire									
Gasser-Kropatschek	9mm	9 G-K	230	120	–	–	770	6	245
Rast & Gasser	8mm	8 R&G	226	117	4	R	900	8	240
Roth-Steyr 1907	8mm	8 Roth	233	131	4	R	1020	10	332
Steyr 1911	9mm	9 Steyr	216	128	4	R	990	8	335
Frommer 1912	7.65mm	7.65 ACP	165	95	4	R	610	7	280
Belgium									
Nagant Offrs '78	9mm	9 Bel Nag	245	140	4	L	950	6	240
Nagant Tprs	9mm	9 Bel Nag	245	140	4	L	950	6	240
Browning M1900	7.65mm	7.65 ACP	170	101	6	R	620	7	290
Browning M1903	9mm	9 Br Long	203	127	6	R	910	7	320
Browning M1922	7.65mm	7.65 ACP	178	114	6	R	730	9	265
Browning Hi-Power	9mm	9 Para	197	118	4	R	990	13	335
Browning DA	9mm	9 Para	200	118	4	R	850	14	335
Brazil									
M973 Auto	.45	.45 ACP	218	120	4 or 6	R		8	360
China (People's Republic)									
Type 64	7.65mm	7.65 T64	222	95			1810	9	205
Type 67	7.65mm	7.65 T64	225	89			1020	9	181
Czechoslovakia									
CZ24	9mm	9 Br Short	152	91	6	R	700	8	295
CZ27	9mm	9 Br Short	158	100	6	R	700	8	295
CZ38	9mm	9 Br Short	206	118	6	R	940	8	300
CZ50	7.65mm	7.65 ACP	167	94	6	R	660	8	285
CZ52	7.62mm	7.62 Soviet	209	120	4	R	880	8	395
CZ75	9mm	9 Para	210	122	4	R	1090	15	338
CZ83	9mm	9 Makarov	173	96	6	R	650	12	340

Name	Calibre	Cartridge	Overall length (mm)	Barrel length (mm)	Rifling grooves	Rifling twist	Weight empty (gm)	Magazine capacity	Muzzle velocity (m/sec)
Denmark									
Ronge Navy	9mm	9 Danish	260	137	–	–	900	6	200
Bergmann M1910	9mm	9 Berg-Bay	254	101	4	L	1020	10	395
Egypt									
Tokagypt	9mm	9 Para	194	114	6	R	910	7	350
Finland									
Lahti M35	9mm	9 Para	245	105	6	R	1220	8	350
France									
Modèle 1873	11mm	11 Fr Ord	242	113	6	R	1195	6	245
Modèle 1892	8mm	8 M92	236	117	6	R	840	6	228
Ruby	7.65mm	7.65 ACP	155	88	4	R	665	9	285
SACM M35A	7.65mm	7.65 Long	189	109	4	R	730	8	305
MAC M35S	7.65mm	7.65 Long	189	109	4	R	730	8	305
MAS M50	9mm	9mm Para	192	112	4	R	680	9	335
MAB PA-15	9mm	9mm Para	203	117	4	R	1070	15	350
Germany (to 1945)									
Reichsrev '79	10.6mm	10.6 Ger	310	183	6	R	1040	6	205
Reichsrev '83	10.6mm	10.6 Ger	260	126	6	R	940	6	195
Mauser C/96	7.63mm	7.63 Maus	312	139	4 or 6	R	1250	10	434
Schwarzlose	7.63mm	7.63 Maus	273	163	4	R	940	7	426
Pistole '04	9mm	9 Para	267	152	4	R	960	8	366
Pistole '08	9mm	9 Para	223	102	6	R	870	8	350
Pist Long '08	9mm	9 Para	311	190	6	R	1050	8 or 32	380
Langenhan	7.65mm	7.65 ACP	168	105	4	R	650	8	280
Beholla	7.65mm	7.65 ACP	140	73	6	R	640	7	275
Sauer 'Old'	7.65mm	7.65 ACP	144	75	6	R	570	7	275
Walther PP	7.65mm	7.65 ACP	162	85	6	R	710	8	290
Walther PPK	7.65mm	7.65 ACP	148	80	6	R	590	7	285
Sauer 38	7.65mm	7.65 ACP	171	83	4	R	700	8	290
Mauser HsC	7.65mm	7.65 ACP	152	86	6	RH	600	8	290
Pistole '38	9mm	9 Para	213	127	6	R	840	8	350
Germany (Federal Republic)									
Walther P1	9mm	9 Para	218	124	6	R	772	8	350
H&K P7	9mm	9 Para	166	105	4 Poly	R	800	8 or 13	338
Great Britain									
Enfield Mks I, II	.476	.476 Enfield	291	143	7	R	1148	6	205
Webley I	.476	.476 Enfield	235	101	6	R	990	6	183
Webley II	.442	.442 Eley	235	101	7	R	995	6	215
Webley III	.455	.455 Svc	241	101	7	R	1048	6	185
Webley IV	.455	.455 Svc	235	101	7	R	1020	6	215

Name	Calibre	Cartridge	Overall length (mm)	Barrel length (mm)	Rifling grooves	Rifling twist	Weight empty (gm)	Magazine capacity	Muzzle velocity (m/sec)
Webley V	.455	.455 Svc	235	101	7	R	1005	6	215
Webley VI	.455	.455 Svc	286	152	7	R	1077	6	230
Webley-Fosbery	.455	.455 Svc	280	152	7	R	1240	6	185
Webley & Scott	.455	.455 W&S Auto	216	127	6	R	1130	7	228
Smith & Wesson	.455	.455 Svc	298	165			1077	6	240
Garate OP No 1	.455	.455 Svc	280	130	6	R	680	6	200
Trocaola OP No 2	.455	.455 Svc	280	130	6	R	680	6	200
Enfield No 2	.38	.38 Svc	260	127	7	R	760	6	198
Webley IV	.38	.38 Svc	266	127	7	R	760	6	183

Hungary

Frommer M29	9mm	9 Br Short	172	100	4	R	750	7	270
Frommer M37	7.65mm	7.65 ACP	182	110	6	R	770	7	280
Walam M/48	7.65mm	7.65 ACP	175	100	4	R	700	8	290

Israel

Revolver	9mm	9mm Para	279	155	6	R	862	6	350

Italy

Cham-Delvigne	10.4mm	10.4 Ital	279	156	4	R	1135	6	255
Bodeo	10.4mm	10.4 Ital	235	114			950	6	240
Glisenti M910	9mm	9 Glis	207	100	6	R	820	7	320
Beretta M915	7.65mm	7.65 ACP	149	84	6	R	570	8	295
Beretta M922	7.65mm	7.65 ACP	146	87	4	R	670	7	297
Beretta M934	9mm	9 Br Short	152	94	4	R	660	7	250
Beretta M851	9mm	9 Para	203	114	6	R	890	8	395
Beretta M93R	9mm	9 Para	240	156	6	R	1120	15 or 20	375
Beretta M92	9mm	9 Para	217	125	6	R	1000	15	340

Japan

Type 26	9mm	9 Japan	216	120	6	L	880	6	230
Nambu 4th	8mm	8 Nambu	220	120	6	R	900	8	335
Nambu 14th	8mm	8 Nambu	227	121	6	R	900	8	320
Baby Nambu	7mm	7 Nambu	171	83	6	R	650	7	305
Type 94	8mm	8 Nambu	180	79	6	R	790	6	305
New Nambu 57A	9mm	9 Para	198	118	6	R	900	8	350

Mexico

Obregon	.45	.45 ACP	210	124	6	R	1020	7	260

Netherlands

Cham-Delv '73	9.4mm	9.4 Dutch	280	161	6	R	1300	6	180
KNIL '91	9.4mm	9.4 Dutch	222	113	4	R	825	6	155

Poland

Radom	9mm	9 Para	211	115	6	R	1050	8	350

Name	Calibre	Cartridge	Overall length (mm)	Barrel length (mm)	Rifling grooves	Rifling twist	Weight empty (gm)	Magazine capacity	Muzzle velocity (m/sec)
PM-63	9mm	9 Makarov	162	85	4	R	610	6	300
Portugal									
Abadie Offrs	9.1mm	9.1 Abadie	218	113	4	L	752	6	162
Abadie Tprs	9.1mm	9.1 Abadie	250	142	4	L	835	6	178
Savage M915	7.65mm	7.65 ACP	167	87	4	R	570	10	290
Spain									
Berg-Bayard	9mm	9 Largo	254	102	6	R	1020	10	340
Campo-Giro	9mm	9 Largo	204	165	6	R	960	8	355
Astra 400	9mm	9 Largo	235	140	6	R	1080	8	343
Astra 300	7.65mm	7.65 ACP	165	90	6	R	560	7	300
Star B	9mm	9 Para	222	130	4	R	1020	8	400
Star 28DA	9mm	9 Para	205	110	4	R	1140	15	350
Astra A-80	9mm	9 Para	180	97	4	R	980	15	350
Sweden									
Nagant	7.5mm	7.5 Nagant	230	112	4	R	830	6	223
Lahti M/40	9mm	9 Para	272	140	4	R	1100	8	390
Switzerland									
Cham-Delvigne	10.4mm	10.4 RF	275	150	6	R	1000	6	175
Schmidt	10.4mm	10.4 Swiss	235	116	4	R	750	6	185
Schmidt	7.5mm	7.5 Swiss	235	116	4	R	750	6	220
Parabellum	7.65mm	7.65 Para	237	120	4	R	890	8	350
SIG P-210	9mm	9 Para	215	120	6	R	990	8	350
SIG P-220	9mm	9 Para	198	112	6	R	810	9	345
SIG P-225	9mm	9 Para	180	131	6	R	790	8	345
SIG P-226	9mm	9 Para	196	112	6	R	840	15	350
SIG P-230	9mm	9 Police	168	92	6	R	690	7	320
USA									
Colt SA Army	.45	.45 Colt	260	120	6	L	1020	6	265
S&W Schofield	.45	.45 S&W	315	178	5	R	1142	6	225
Colt DA Army	.45	.45 Colt	316	190	6	L	1105	6	280
Colt New Army	.38	.38 Colt	292	152	6	L	937	6	235
S&W Hand Ejec	.38	.38 Colt	230	101	5	R	875	6	235
Colt New Service	.45	.45 Colt	248	114	6	L	1105	6	255
Colt M1911/11A1	.45	.45 ACP	216	127	6	L	1130	7	262
Colt M1917	.45	.45 ACP	272	140	6	L	1140	6	260
S&W M1917	.45	.45 ACP	274	140	6	R	1020	6	260
Colt Gen Offrs	.45	.45 ACP	200	106	6	L	1030	7	245
M9 (Beretta 92F)	9mm	9 Para	217	125	6	R	950	15	390

Name	Calibre	Cartridge	Overall length (mm)	Barrel length (mm)	Rifling grooves	Rifling twist	Weight empty (gm)	Magazine capacity	Muzzle velocity (m/sec)
USSR/Russia									
S&W Russian	.44	.44 Russian	305	165	5	R	1135	6	198
Nagant M95	7.62mm	7.62 Nagant	229	110	4	R	790	7	305
Mauser Bolo	7.63mm	7.63 Maus	218	99	4	R	1100	10	425
Tokarev TT-33	7.62mm	7.62 Soviet	193	116	4	R	830	8	415
Makarov	9mm	9 Makarov	160	91	4	R	663	8	315
Stechkin	9mm	9 Makarov	225	127	4	R	1030	20	340
PSM	5.45mm	5.45 Soviet	160	85	6	R	460	8	315
Yugoslavia									
Model M70(d)	9mm	9 Para	200	116	6	R	910	9	330
Model M70(k)	9mm	9 Br Short	200	94	6	R	720	8	260

Abbreviations and Special Terms used in this Table

ACP	Automatic Colt Pistol (cartridge)	Fr Ord	French Ordnance (cartridge)	Offrs	Officers'
		Ger	German Ordnance (cartridge)	OP	Old Pattern
Bel Nag	Belgian Nagant (cartridge)			Para	Parabellum (cartridge)
Berg-Bay	Bergmann-Bayard (cartridge)	G-K	Gasser-Kropatschek (cartridge)	Poly	Polygonal rifling
				RF	Rimfire
Br Long	Browning Long (cartridge)	Glis	Glisenti (cartridge)	R&G	Rast & Gasser (cartridge)
Br Short	Browning Short (cartridge)	Ital	Italian Ordnance (cartridge)	Svc	Service pattern (cartridge)
DA	Double Action	Mann	Mannlicher	T64	Type 64 (cartridge)
		Maus	Mauser	Tprs	Troopers'
				W&S	Webley & Scott

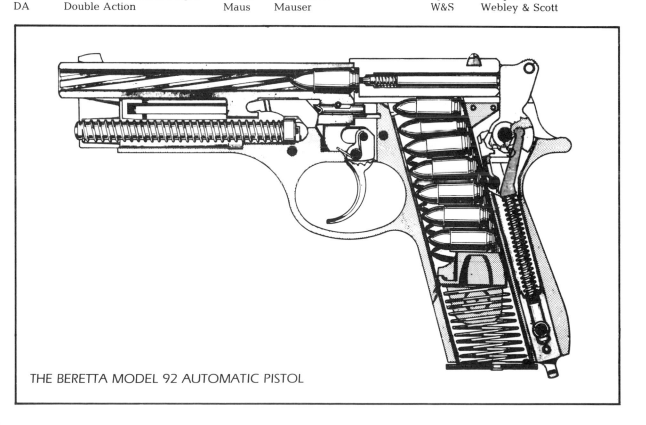

THE BERETTA MODEL 92 AUTOMATIC PISTOL

APPENDIX 3
SERVICE PISTOL AMMUNITION DATA

Calibre and title	Round length (mm)	Case length (mm)	Rim dia. (mm)	Bullet weight (gm)	Muzzle velocity (m/sec)
5.45mm Soviet	24.9	17.8	7.5	2.6	315
7mm Nambu	27.0	19.7	9.1	3.5	320
7.5mm Nagant	33.0	22.7	10.3	6.8	225
7.5mm Swiss	35.2	22.5	10.2	6.8	221
7.62mm Nagant	38.8	38.8	10.3	7.0	290
7.62mm Soviet	35.1	25.2	9.9	5.6	455
7.63mm Mannlicher	28.5	21.0	8.8	5.6	312
7.63mm Mauser	34.6	25.0	9.9	5.7	443
7.65mm ACP	25.0	17.0	9.0	5.0	300
7.65mm French Long	30.2	19.8	8.6	5.5	366
7.65mm Parabellum	29.9	21.6	9.9	6.0	368
7.65mm Type 64	24.0	17.0	8.5	6.3	205
8mm French Ord M92	36.5	27.0	10.3	9.5	260
8mm Nambu	31.7	21.5	10.5	6.5	325
8mm Rast & Gasser	36.0	27.0	9.6	7.8	240
8mm Roth	31.0	20.8	8.9	7.5	270
9mm Belgian Nagant	34.0	22.4	12.2	12.1	240
9mm Berg-Bayard (Largo)	33.5	23.1	9.9	8.8	340
9mm Browning Short	25.0	17.3	9.5	6.2	270
9mm Browning Long	27.7	20.0	10.3	7.2	335
9mm Danish	27.3	17.0	11.0	8.0	200
9mm Gasser-Kropatschek	33.8	26.0	11.2	10.4	245
9mm Glisenti	29.0	19.0	9.9	8.1	320
9mm Japanese revolver	29.5	22.0	11.0	9.7	195
9mm Makarov	24.8	18.0	10.0	6.0	340
9mm Parabellum	29.7	19.2	10.0	7.5	396
9mm Police	25.5	18.0	9.5	6.1	345
9mm Steyr	33.0	23.0	9.7	7.5	361
9.1mm Abadie	27.3	17.5	11.0	8.3	162
9.4mm Dutch	31.0	21.0	12.4	12.9	180
10.4mm Italian	29.7	19.7	13.2	11.4	255
10.4 Swiss	31.7	20.0	13.5	12.5	185
10.6mm German	36.0	24.7	13.0	17.0	205
11mm French Ord	30.0	17.7	12.5	11.0	245
.38 British	31.6	19.4	11.0	12.9	180
.38 Long Colt	34.4	26.2	11.1	10.0	240
.38 S&W	32.0	19.5	10.7	9.4	215
.44 Russian	36.0	24.0	12.9	15.0	235
.442 Eley	30.0	17.0	12.7	14.0	212
.45 ACP	32.4	22.8	12.0	15.2	250
.45 Auto-Rim	32.8	22.7	13.0	14.9	250
.45 Colt	41.0	32.0	13.0	16.2	265
.45 S&W Schofield	36.2	28.3	13.2	16.4	235
.455 British	36.5	21.8	13.5	17.2	216
.455 Webley Auto	31.0	23.3	12.7	14.5	225
.476 Enfield	37.7	22.0	13.4	17.5	220

NOTES:
1. Dimensions are based on an average of several rounds where possible, on a single round in the case of older types, and may show small differences from other specimens. The amount of tolerance permitted varies, and will usually be found to be larger in older types.
2. Muzzle velocities are official manufacturers' figures and may have been determined in test barrels rather than in service weapons. They may therefore differ by a small amount from the values given in Appendix 2.

INDEX